TAKE ME
WITH YOU

TALES OF LONG DISTANCE LOVE

2/1/07 To my baby,
I Love you so much
& want you to
remember I'll
always ♡
you !!

Your Lachlan

TAKE ME WITH YOU

TALES OF LONG DISTANCE LOVE

EDITED BY SARAH MACDONALD

BANTAM
SYDNEY AUCKLAND TORONTO NEW YORK LONDON

TAKE ME WITH YOU
A BANTAM BOOK

First published in Australia and New Zealand in 2005 by Bantam

Quotation from *Conversations at Curlow Creek* by David Malouf in
'Letters to a Faraway Land' reproduced by permission of the author.

National Library of Australia
Cataloguing-in-Publication Entry

Take me with you: tales of long distance love.

ISBN 1 86325 556 7.

1. Travelers' writings, Australian. 2. Voyages and travels.
3. Australians – Travel. I. Macdonald, Sarah.

910.4

Transworld Publishers,
a division of Random House Australia Pty Ltd
20 Alfred Street, Milsons Point, NSW 2061
http://www.randomhouse.com.au

Random House New Zealand Limited
18 Poland Road, Glenfield, Auckland

Transworld Publishers,
a division of The Random House Group Ltd
61–63 Uxbridge Road, Ealing, London W5 5SA

Random House Inc.
1745 Broadway, New York, New York 10036

Cover design by Christabella Designs
Internal design by Darian Causby/www.highway51.com.au
Cover image courtesy Australian Picture Library
Typeset by Midland Typesetters, Australia
Printed and bound by Griffin Press, Netley, South Australia

10 9 8 7 6 5 4 3 2 1

Contents

Introduction

By the time I was 21 I was ready to take on the world. I had one year, one round-the-world ticket, one backpack and one aim: to escape my home, family and suburban life for a world of carefree independence. I had arranged to travel with two of my friends – one based in Sydney, the other in the UK. Then potential disaster struck. Suddenly and simultaneously, on opposite sides of the globe, they each met a boy and fell madly in love.

I was not surprised – so many people I knew found romance just before hitting the road. Each had a different theory as to why it happened that way. Some thought it was the cruel hand of fate; others believed it was cupid testing love's mettle. I believed it was because for a young bloke there's nothing as irresistible as a girl with the gleam of adventure in her eye and a ticket in her hand.

Whatever the reason, it was shocking timing. I already

had a boyfriend and was hoping my friends would yank me free of his anchor and keep my mind fixed on the business of backpacking.

Their new love affairs didn't stop my mates coming with me but it did mean they were less adventurous than I had hoped. In the wonderfully strange places we travelled to we all spent far too much of our time longing for the familiarity of our boys. Our year of freedom and discovery was accompanied by lovers' ghosts.

Many years after my backpacker trawl I fell in love with someone who was about to go overseas for work. As Jonathan and I prepared to endure the time apart it seemed everyone I knew had been through the 'distance thing' and all had advice on how to survive it. In this age of cheap travel and international business it's inevitable that many people will experience long distance love in some form or other. And while increased connections make the world seem smaller, the loss, longing and lust of those who yearn for another ensure it's never small enough.

Hence this book.

Take Me With You explores the agony and the ecstasy of love lived from afar.

Tom Gleeson is accustomed to abandoning his girlfriend to gallivant around the countryside on comedy gigs. In 'The Italian Job' that situation is reversed. His story reveals the danger of being left alone too long to indulge in romantic fantasies.

I'd always assumed it was harder to be the one left

behind. But in 'Better Than Barry' I find a sweet taste in the sadness of home, and a richness in everyday life that distance can bring.

As a UN interpreter Valerie Barnes experiences the sadness of separation and the intense joy of clandestine reunions in many different countries. Her relationship doesn't just have to conquer distance, but also misunderstandings about slang in Australia and alcohol in Japan.

When distance is conquered, success is sweet – but it cannot always erase the pain of separation. Long distance love is nearly always laced with a sense of loss.

In the story 'In an Old Frame' Kendall Hill makes a pilgrimage to Greece to mourn a mate killed in an accident. It's a haunting ode to friendships that we forge in our youth – relationships that inevitably change due to distance, the passage of time and our growing up.

Mandy Sayer writes about the loss of her beloved father. Yet as death creeps closer a tender new love is born. After sadness there is joy. After rupture there is union. But for Mandy, this new relationship of shared passions and peculiar differences is best experienced a short distance apart.

Love can fail when it's lived too close. Emily Ballou comes to Australia to be with her lover, only to discover that a relationship built on separateness cannot survive constant togetherness. In 'Letters to a Faraway Land' she grows exuberant when her move leads to another love – for a place.

Nicholas Hope cannot love the land onto which he is

transplanted. It hurts his heart. 'Heartache' reveals the complications of a relationship lived in a place that is home to one and alien to the other. Nicholas and his partner are only exotic to each other when experienced out of context.

Passion *can* survive a permanent move apart. In 'The Lost City' John Birmingham writes a love letter to a feckless tart he left only reluctantly. At times, John's so lovesick he lives in denial, pretending he is still with his beloved, when Sydney has forgotten he even exists.

Sarah Darmody discovers how time and distance distort relationships. Revisiting Borneo with her new love brings about a clash between her past and her present. Sarah mourns the loss of her childhood life and spirit.

All relationships require words but in those lived apart the written word is vital. It's the oxygen long distance love needs to survive. As Emily Ballou puts it, in reference to letter writing, it's 'the sigh of a soul'. I hope the writings contained in this collection will swell your heart, especially if you have suffered the pain of separation, the exquisite thrill of reunion and the comfort – or tension – of togetherness.

Here's to the triumph of love. May it ever conquer the kilometres it must cross!

Sarah Macdonald

Better than Barry

SARAH MACDONALD

How I expected to pick up the love of my life while dressed as the slutty Spice Girl Ginger, God only knows. But I was feeling confident and, to be honest, a little cocky. It seemed none of my friends had noticed that it was the third year in a row I'd invited them to my thirtieth birthday party. (I found out recently they *had* realised but were humouring me.) It was June 1998 and I was co-hosting the party with five fellow Gemini chicks. For the invitation we plastered photos of our heads on the Spice Girls' bodies. Then, while planning the shindig, one of us (perhaps it was me and I've wiped the memory to save face) had the harebrained idea of performing a midnight show for our guests. We hired the Spice Girls movie and learnt the moves to the song 'Spice Up Your Life'. Easy choreography, an easy laugh – and, I thought, an easy way to impress Jonathan.

Jonathan was the boy next door, a valley and one beach removed. He lived in a terrace house on the hill above Bronte, in Sydney, and I lived near the Tamarama gully. I'd seen him around over the past few years. I'd known him well enough to be aware that he had been, until a year before, in a relationship, but not well enough to know he was perfect for a future relationship with *me*. Until, newly single after a long relationship with someone I loved dearly but had absolutely nothing in common with, I grew slowly entranced by Jonathan. By the time the Spice Girls dance party came along we were midway through a two-month waltz around each other – neither of us willing to make the first move. So I decided that on this night of nights I would activate girl power Spice style. I wiggled into a black sixties swimming costume with net over the navel and pointy boobs, teamed it with knee-high boots and a red wig and made a few Spicy moves on him.

At midnight we Gemini Spice Girls gathered in the change room preparing for our performance. Sporty Spice got stage fright and threw a diva act.

'I can't do it. It's too embarrassing. I'll never live it down.'

The others encouraged her warmly.

'It'll be fun.'

'Don't worry.'

'Don't be silly.'

But I jumped on her like a promoter about to lose his millions.

'Come on. Don't be a wimp. We have to do it!' I yelled, pulling her off the bench. I was getting desperate. So far that night Jonathan had been impervious to my flirting. We'd had one dance together to a Barry White number but now it looked like he was going to head for the exit.

The crowd outside was growing restless. The DJ had stopped the music. A slow clapping began. With the help of a shot of something, Sporty gave in. We jumped out from behind a curtain and strutted our stuff. The crowd was, initially, silent with shock. But soon, our friends, families and assorted gatecrashers were screaming and running towards us. Some were clapping, others whistling; most were dancing and a few were prostrating themselves at our feet. I only wanted to see the reaction of one person. I scanned the crowd. It was as if a spotlight fell on Jonathan. He was staring at me, mouth open, eyes wide.

Ten minutes later he left.

I was bummed. Not to mention humiliated. I was growing increasingly convinced he was the guy for me. I had always known he was kind, considerate, funny and exuberant. But slowly he was revealing a hilarious, beautiful, passionate and thoughtful soul. We bumped into each other every Saturday at a café where mutual friends held forth at a communal table. Over the weeks I found out that he once ran a green bookshop and a drop-in centre, that he was involved in an international youth group for social change, and that he had bonded so well with Ben Harper that the musician had been in his car! One Saturday he dropped in to pick up a take-away coffee and a milkshake, with his four-year-old nephew bouncing atop his shoulders. I was impressed that Jonathan had taken Sam for a swim on the beach and was now escorting him to inspect the ABC helicopter, but I was astounded when Uncle Jonathan revealed he wasn't just babysitting for the day but the entire weekend.

And then there was the music. I had loved someone who loved rock. I had loved someone who loved disco. I had loved someone who loved funk. I'd never loved someone who loved all three.

Jonathan did. The problem was that I soon found out he loved the idea of adventure more than he loved me.

Well, that's exaggerating a bit. He didn't really love disco (with the exception of that crooner of 'lurve' Barry White). But he had been offered the title of ABC South Asia correspondent based in India – a dream position that offered travel, excitement and a career trajectory. He'd left my Spice Girls party to be sparky for the interview a day later. While on our first date two weeks after that, he mentioned he'd applied. I chose to agree with Jonathan that he probably didn't stand a chance of success. A week later we were an item. We'd been together for three weeks when he was offered the job, before he even knew if what we had was a relationship or just a romance. He couldn't turn down the job of a lifetime for a possibility. And I couldn't quit my job to join him without looking desperate or mad or desperately mad.

My job involved music. I was a Sydney announcer at the national radio station Triple J. While I hosted a magazine-style show with lots of talk, Triple J is, at its core, a music station. I got to interview rock stars, go backstage, take home free CDs. My job and its music defined me. Made friendships. Provided a social life and gave me a small ounce of credibility in a city that seeks status. (The Spice Girls act was a tongue-in-cheek piss-take.) I loved music. I loved the fact that Jonathan and I loved the same music.

I knew music could be shared long distance. I just wasn't sure love could.

I'd done long distance love three times and I'd vowed I would never do it again. The first time I was twenty-one and left my first long-term boyfriend (the one who loved rock) for Europe; I wasted much of my time away missing him. I couldn't get him out of my head while I was swimming on the Greek Islands, eating my way around Italian cities and rubbernecking communist lives in East Germany's bullet-scarred streets. When I returned home a year later I realised a rare opportunity for me to be alone, free and reckless was gone. I resented the fact that he'd been with me in spirit. So, as an act of revenge, I dumped him.

In my second experience of long distance love I was left bereft in Sydney when my disco-loving boy moved away. For a week I howled along the wind-battered seashore, my tears mixing with salt spray. The next week

I set my radio to classic hits and sang along to tragic love songs with huge abandonment and volume. The third week I fell in love with a boy who loved funk.

Seven months later, I moved to Canberra to be Triple J's political reporter. A week later his voice blurted from the office answering machine: 'Hi, it's me, um, you won't believe this but last night a coffee plunger exploded and burnt my penis. Don't worry. I've done a wee this morning, it works, but it kills. Wish you were here.' I grimaced. But a carpenter who had come in to build me a studio got down from his ladder to rock with pain. He said, 'Geez love, you should be there with him, he needs you.' I didn't go. Much later he admitted his love died about then.

But maybe long distance could work with Jonathan. He liked Massive Attack, U2, Luka Bloom and Barry White. He preferred his coffee percolated. We had been friends before we were lovers. I admired him, I respected him, I trusted him, I loved his enthusiasm for life and I could really talk to him. And, it turned out that once he recovered from the shock he didn't get turned off by the Spice Girls thing. This guy was brave!

Before he accepted the job we decided we should talk maturely about our options. We lay on the grassy hill above Bondi Beach, two bleary-eyed lovers staring over the sea, feeling like shy strangers. Around us British backpackers burped on beer, beat boxes boomed, South American boys twisted their bodies into positions of pose and poise, and the skateboarders ground relentlessly up and down their ramp. The distance between us stretched with what we didn't say. He didn't say, 'Come.' I didn't say, 'Don't go.' Such demands were impossible to make on a partner of less than a month, but in a way we both wanted to hear them. And yet, we would have been terrified if the other had agreed to them. Our partnership was too new, too raw, to be burdened with responsibility and sacrifice.

'I think we should try the long distance thing,' he said.

'Yes,' I answered. Flatly.

'But it can't be endless. We need to limit it.' Jonathan spoke quietly, almost hesitantly.

I did not hesitate.

'Let's give it a year and then one of us will move,' I suggested, suspecting it would be me, and oddly not infuriated by the idea.

We both sighed.

'That's the price I pay –' I began to sing.

'For loving you the way that I do,' he finished.

And that's when I decided to really risk it. Anyone who can quote Billy Bragg at such a moment must be worth a shot.

The best songs have a slow build. They start soft and build up and up so gradually that you don't know the mood of the song has changed until you are belting along the highway yelling the words out to the wind. Our relationship had had a slow build. Torturously slow. Neither of us had wanted to make the first move. My Spice Girls move had fallen flat; we hadn't wanted to hurt the friendship; we had been confused about each other's signals. When we had finally got together I nearly blew it by responding to his first kiss with, 'Should we be doing this?' When I saw how hurt he looked my heart let go of all the fear; I added, '. . . without Barry?' and put a Barry White CD on the stereo.

But what had taken a long time to get going began to burn furiously after our discussion on the hill at Bondi. We had six months together before he left. Six months to develop habits, routines, secret lovers' language, private jokes, friendships with each other's families, and nicknames. Six months to make that ultimate Sydney commitment – a sharing of real estate.

Six months. Just enough time to fall more deeply in love. But not enough time to see if we were really companionable. Not enough time to notice each other's annoying habits or to get bored. Just enough time to set each other up for more hurt. But we did it anyway. Love makes you adventurous, willing to take risks. Reckless with your heart.

Why is it that people so often fall in love just before one of them is going away?

We spent the last few weeks before Jonathan left taking a road trip south. We had both been north many times before and wanted to stamp new territory together. We were stupidly optimistic about an early summer and moronically optimistic about our vehicle: the coolest car I had ever bought, a 1966 powder-blue Ford Falcon with streamlined fins. We cuddled up on the bench seat and felt so very cool as we left Sydney's endless ring of suburbia. But we got hot and cranky fast, breaking down three times before we even got to the Great Ocean Road. The road romance was almost murdered when the car died in the aptly named town of Kilmore, where it was so hot the asphalt melted my thongs and the pub gave off a warm cloud of vaporised cigarette trampled into spilt beer. The engine needed major repairs. We ended up in a tow truck to Melbourne. I squatted in the bed trying not to let any of the exposed skin on my legs touch the filthy Thomas the Tank Engine sheets. Jonathan sat in the front trying to ignore the driver's rant about varieties of road kill. It's never sexy seeing your partner furious.

Still, before Melbourne, there were long lovely nights in ocean-view hotel rooms with whipped concrete ceilings, listening to the swish of traffic. Wrapped in lime-green chenille bedspreads, we watched videos while wet winds slapped tree branches against the window of our bed and breakfast at Wilsons Promontory. We sang along to music on my crappy car tape deck. We shared cheese-and-ham toasties and chocolate milkshakes in small-town cafés. At a place still named Blackfellows Point I taught Jonathan to do cartwheels on a deserted beach of damp sand and cold brewing sea. At Pebbly Beach we shared a camping ground with kangaroos that pestered us like seagulls. Near Orbost we trampled across paddocks dotted with limpid-eyed cows, and through wet wilderness that seemed to drip with our approaching sorrow.

Back in Sydney we fitted our final moments together around Jonathan's camera training sessions, removal vans and the selling of his car. Our remaining time grew so precious that we spent much of his going-away party wishing everyone would leave. At 2 am we were so desperate to be alone we called the police and asked them to shut us down. On our last day we took over the communal table at our favourite café. Jonathan faced the sea he'd miss and the neighbourhood he loved. I faced him, my back to the Norfolk Island pines, the black four-wheel drives, the picnics, the playground and the ball games. His friends dropped by to wish him well; the conversation, hugs and jibes revealed a forced joviality. I sat with rising edginess from the caffeine and a growing lump in my throat. I didn't want to share him in these last moments and yet I felt so proud of him.

And now.

It's the night before he leaves. A night we don't want to waste on tears. We have tickets to the musical about Peter Allen, *The Boy From Oz*, so we go. We are the youngest in the audience by a good twenty years; I've never seen so many wheelchairs in one place at one time. During the scene in which Peter rings his mum and reveals his homosexuality the old lady behind us gasps for air and retches, her arms flailing. Jonathan tenses, ready to respond with CPR. I wonder what heart-stopping surprises are in store for *us*. What shocks we will communicate by phone. What the world will reveal about Jonathan. Will long distance love shatter the image of my ideal man?

At midnight Jonathan gives me two books. The pages are blank. 'How romantic,' I say, sarcastically.

'Long distance love books,' he replies, taking one back. 'We'll write in them whenever we want and swap them around when we see each other. Purge. Put in it what you dare not say on the phone, what you forget to put in letters. What is too personal for emails, what you know you'll forget if you don't jot it down.'

I give him a photo of his favourite place: the seaside rock pool where he swims every morning, all year round. I'd asked a friend to take it a few months before. In the photo it is dusk on a cold spring night. The full moon is rising – bright like the sun, clearly defined against air blown clean. The indigo sky meets the inky-black sea in sharp relief; the rocks are a soft violet. The surf is phos-phorescent and appears like a mist, swirling around the rusting yellow council sign. I can see the same pool from my window and I tell him to look at his photo every after-noon when I'll be looking at the real thing. We'll be linked through the pool. Only I will be able to swim in it, to smell its seaweed stains, to feel its oily layer of sunscreen and taste its brine; and only I will see how it changes over the seasons. He'll have to experience those things through me.

When he sees the photo Jonathan cries. And when he leaves in the morning he cries again. I have been sobbing for days but when he actually walks through customs, his shoulders so stooped and so heavy, I feel a strange calm. I decide it is better to be left than to leave. While he will be alone in a foreign country I will be able to find comfort in friends, the familiarity of daily routines and the rituals we once shared. I decide to make use of this advantage early: at the airport I invite a group of his mates to return to my flat for a feast from the local Russian Deli – smoked salmon, sour cream, Polish mushrooms, toast, coffee, mango and watermelon. I eat the food he likes and drink his drink – vodka, lime and soda. After everyone leaves I still don't feel alone. It's as if he is still hovering over my left shoulder. A few times I even begin to talk to him. Before bed I watch his pool – the bright green waves have a creamy white sheen and they crash under a heavy grey summer sky. He's left me his Style Council CD box set – I put 'Headstart for Happiness' on the stereo.

I awake the next morning scratchy-eyed and hollow in a bed that still smells like him. I wander around the flat feeling his absence and hating the silence. By ten, less than twenty-four hours after he's left, I've changed my mind: it's worse to be left. His new life will be refreshingly empty of me, while mine will be full of the void where he used to be. Everything reminds me of him: the food I eat, the coffee I drink, the view of the sea that I love. I indulge in the feeling of sadness and enjoy the delicious romantic taste of the tears. Yet, in that funk,

I realise I feel loved, cherished and protected by Jonathan even when we are apart. I've been in relationships with other men in which I didn't feel such confidence and comfort when we were in the same room. This thought cheers me. To further wash away the pain I do something that gives Jonathan pleasure: I swim laps of his pool (eight for each of us). I float on my back with the sun harsh in my eyes and I kick, making diamond droplets in the air. Buoyancy returns to me in waves.

I decide I will use this year to learn to love being alone. I am a serial monogamist. I need to know that if Jonathan and I end up together it is because I want it, not need it.

But it is the beginning of summer, the party season when new relationships flower into love. It's the time when people start walking pelvis first, their sexual swagger showing availability and that frisky feeling. It's a time of needs. It's not a time to be left alone.

My life and Jonathan's life, which had been so similar, become dramatically different. I embrace Sydney's frenzy of consumerism by going Christmas shopping. I bob in a pool of harassed mums, screaming kids, sweaty business-men and gaggles of teenage girls in black, while being serenaded by muzak. He sits alone in an echoing apart-ment with no one to shop for, and the sound of mad Indian traffic and high-pitched Hindi movie classics blasting through his window. I dance at summer music festivals, bouncing off sweaty beautiful bodies; he walks past living skeletons in slums that are so crowded no

one even gets to shit alone. He is plunged into stories
of death, disaster and danger while I sit on a beach
surrounded by the residue of frivolity: cigarette butts,
Gatorade bottles, skinny glamorous girls in G-strings,
and hairless beefcakes in Speedos and mirror glasses. At
night I fall asleep to the swish of the waves on the sand,
the song of cicadas and the occasional blast of a car
stereo. His lullaby is a highway of metal and men and
the buzz of a billion lives. He works, at times twenty
hours a day. I am still on summer break – sleeping in,
and staying up late.

One night I join friends at Centennial Park. Bats beat
their wings above us, slick wet joggers pant past us.
Reclining on cushions we eat cold chicken and drink
warm champagne at the open-air cinema. It's a pre-
Christmas viewing of *Life of Brian*. I laugh for Jonathan.
In front of the screen couples cuddle up close and I feel
jealousy stir within me. My arms itch to hold someone. I
feel a touch of sadness that we never had such summer
nights together. When the lights come on the cockroaches
scurry and I hide my tears of sadness and joy from the
glare.

We can still listen to the same music – Morcheeba
provides our summer soundtrack. I blast it from the
stereo while leaning back on my chair, my feet on my salt-
rotted windowsill, vodka at my side. I sing out over the
red-tiled rooftops, the spindles of antennas and the ever-
changing sea as it spills into his pool.

I keep seeing him. Everywhere. At the beach my heart

leaps at the sight of a spiky head; at a party I'll miss a breath when I see a flash of a toothy grin. For a split second I imagine he has flown home to surprise me – then reality hits. I don't get too despondent about these let-downs because in some ways Jonathan is always with me. At times I have two-part conversations: one with my companions, the other inside my head with Jonathan. It's easy for me to imagine his replies because we are in contact so often that I have detailed knowledge about his life and state of mind. I write long letters and pages and pages in the book he gave me, while the moths burn up on my bedside light. He sends me descriptions and drawings of the ABC flat, his job and his life. He sends me flowers every month on our anniversary; I take them to my bedroom at night so they are the first thing I see when I wake up. I can't bear it when they begin to die, and I wait until their sweet rot fills the air before I throw them out.

For a New Year's present I send him a photo of us on our road trip, mounted in a blue plastic frame in the shape of Australia. In the photo we are in the car, smiling, our elbows sticking out the window with Aussie cocky confidence.

And of course I send him music. At first I send newly released songs he can't hear in Bollywood-musical-obsessed India, and then as time and distance increases my nerve and my corn factor, mixed minidiscs full of badly hidden meanings: the Carpenters' 'We've Only Just Begun', Peter Allen's 'Tenterfield Saddler', Wings's

'Silly Love Songs'. All just new ways of saying the same things: I miss you, I want you, I love you. That mantra of all long distance lovers that is never original but always the cause of a uniquely bittersweet funk.

In February Sydney gets monsoon muggy. The air is thick and huge clouds spill sudden buckets of rain; steam rises from the pavements and the sea is choppy and grey, bobbing with butts, plastic bags, condoms and dog shit. The romance of the long distance romance gets lost in the muck. Weekends are the worst times. I grow tetchy with too much spare time for moping; he grows tired and cranky with not enough. We feel helpless to support each other through these bad patches. Talking only resolves so much. Sometimes I need him to stroke my hair, or I want to cradle his head in my lap. The heart that felt so enriched by his love begins to scar.

Jonathan's heart is exposed to more physical dangers. The job of correspondents is to go where there is violence and trouble; to prepare him, the ABC sends him to a war-zone survival course in the UK. He sends me a photo of a London telephone box and there, perched on top, is the photo of us in the Australia frame. He takes it with him everywhere, as a slice of the time when our elbows could touch, a time when we travelled together.

While he is shivering in the snowy British countryside, I spend a warm weekend at a friend's holiday house at Killcare, on the New South Wales Central Coast. I feel as if I am travelling for the two of us, aware of how he must miss this part of his homeland. For both Jonathan and I, the highway up the coast is as familiar as family – a ribbon that has taken us both to countless holidays since before memories began. I want to bottle the feeling of lumpy sand under my back and send it to him. I wish I could draw the rock that arches above me like a wave, its insides carved with honeycomb hollows the colours of burnt toffee and rust. Below me is a bay of coarse sand, blue seas that sparkle silver and crumbly cliffs. I doze to a lullaby of humming speedboats, yelping children, whip birds and the swish of the surf, the squeaks of feet in sandy soil and the empty silence that his presence would fill. I want him to smell and taste my salty, singed skin. I wish he could see through my goggles as I swim – the sand below dappled by light and the mercury-like membrane between sea and sky. In a postcard I brag about the tattoos of summer – the ridge of a bluebottle sting, the nibbles of sea lice and the mosquito-bite lumps.

The card is a photo of the nearby bay. Do I want him to appreciate the gums framing an inlet dotted with boats? Do I want him to laugh cynically at the sight of bush bitten by suburban boxes? Or do I want to make him miss them more, perhaps even hurt him for leaving? Maybe a bit of all these. He sends me a photo of us in the Australia frame placed on a windowsill of a Kashmir houseboat. We look out at a lotus land awash with war.

Often weeks go by and I receive no letters from him, then one day four or so will arrive. At times I ration them, but mostly I rip them all open at once and consume

them greedily. My mood is increasingly erratic, fluctu-
ating like waves stirred up by the tides of distance.
Happiness builds slowly to a crest; I float, feeling brave
and high. Then, without warning, I crash, feeling scared,
helpless, alone. At times I silently play the victim,
churning inside with anger and resentment – damn him
for leaving and putting us through this hardship! Blast
him for setting us such a difficult test so early into our
time together! Of course I tone down my frustration on
the phone but often angry words slip out. He bears them
with quiet stoicism, and this just makes me feel angrier.
And guilty. And ashamed. Jonathan is proving himself a
better person than me. He is never jealous of my easy life.

His face begins to get fuzzy in my mind. I can't
remember his smell.

Summer ends with a huge electrical storm that lights
up the horizon every few minutes with a jagged streak
or a disco flash. It marks a milestone. We are three
months – a quarter of the way – through our year apart.
I watch the storm from my window. The surf smashes
against the cliffs and his pool disappears. I choose our
favourite Faithless CD as a soundtrack and realise that
music now has different meanings for each of us. For
Jonathan songs have become companionship, listened
to on headphones during long uncomfortable car rides,
plane trips and in hotel rooms. The music of Paul Kelly
will forever remind him of a road in Afghanistan littered
with tanks. I, on the other hand, can listen to the song
'Randwick Bells' down the road from the church that

possibly inspired the lyrics. He hears the Beatles and thinks of a market stall in Peshawar; I see my suburban childhood.

The phone rings. It is a friend of Jonathan's, Bob, who has just returned from London. Jonathan stayed at his place a month ago and he has letters and photos from him to give me. I've never met Bob before but he invites me for a drink in half an hour's time. I am excited to talk to a person who has touched Jonathan more recently than I have. As I walk out to the car something hits me hard on the head. I look up to be whacked in the eye. Hail! I jump into the car (despite the fact it failed us so miserably on our holiday I am keen to save it) and park it in my garage. When I get out of the car I have to wait, spread-eagled against the mould-covered garage wall. The sky is teeming with huge hailstones. They are landing with such force that it seems the road is roaring. They bounce down the hill, smashing car windows, shredding leaves and covering the ground in a sea of white ice pebbles. I cower awe-struck, being attacked around the ankles by the bouncing blasting ice balls. When the storm is over I run back up to the flat.

My window, the one I sit in front of every night to look at his pool, the one I was just sitting in front of when the phone rang, has been smashed. The glass has flown across the room to the wall opposite – the force must have been momentous. It would have cut me to shreds.

'Hey, it's Jonathan who saved your life,' Bob says over a beer later. 'I am but his agent.'

This thought opens me up to believing that the protective arms of love can cuddle from afar. In that embrace I feel warmed as the weather cools. How I love this Sydney autumn. The waters are reclaimed by the local surfies in black wetsuits who circle the break like sharks. The sands empty and the beaches glow in the afternoon dusk. The fat-wheeled cars with doof-doof stereos screech out of the car parks for the last time. The sunset from my window becomes streaked in layers of pink and purple blown ragged by new winds. There is a feeling of change, possibility and cleanliness in the air as the cold comes. It feels purer than the decadence of summer. It's a better time to be alone. I begin to enjoy the privileges of being single such as the endless eating of stodgy bad food and staying in flannelette pyjamas until lunchtime. I do what I want when I want. I hire girly movies like *Legally Blonde*. I walk endless hours in the local graveyard, above its broken cliffs and through its overgrown native grasses, past headstones whose names have long weathered away. I sit beside stone angels that glow incandescent in the afternoon light. They guard and comfort the dead. And they guard and comfort me.

How I hate this Sydney autumn. Jonathan's emails become shorter and his letters arrive further apart. It makes me anxious. I know it's unfair of me but distance is sapping my confidence. I can't demand more from him: I may be working ten-hour days, but he does twenty. I have time for yoga, walks, movies, friends and family while his job is all-consuming. He is exhausted by lack of sleep, and by the constant exasperation of life in India. He has no time for himself, for me, for us. It is frustrating to not be able to help him, and the anguish of that frustration sours the longing. And at times I don't want to help. I want him to hear my complaints. It hurts him to be the source of my pain and I instantly regret what I say. Long distance love makes me weak.

India's phone system doesn't help. There are long gaps between words while we each wait for the other to speak, or our conversation tumbles out too fast and we speak over each other. The line often echoes and my own voice bounces back at me loudly while his is distant and thin. Often at a special tender heartfelt moment the line bursts with a sudden screech of deafening static. One day, I'm desperate to tell him what I've just seen: a whale rolling over to show its barnacled belly and waving its fin in the waters off Bondi Beach. I see the creature through Jonathan's eyes, truly understanding the thrill of living in a place where I can watch a whale in city waters, where I can swim at a city beach, where I can afford to rent near headlands like none other on the planet. I rush home to tell him about the whale, laughing with the knowledge of his joy. I dial his number. Can't get through. Nothing unusual. Try again. No connection. Again. A sigh. Again – a grimace. Again – the thrill of telling the story is fading fast. After eleven attempts I give up. The delight in the moment has gone. I sit hugging my legs and whispering the story to myself before bed.

The next day we keep the talk small.

'What did you have for breakfast?' he asks.

'Porridge. What about you?'

'Homemade curd.'

It is boring, sure, but we are finding the best calls come when we don't try to convey too much of the longing, and instead talk of things smaller than whales. Things like the view from our windows, what the neighbour said to Jonathan, snippets from the Indian papers, what I wear to work. These little intimacies are what make our lives unique. It's the small things that reveal so much and are the hardest to retain when apart from one another. Jonathan ends each story with the words, 'and I kept thinking, "Sarah would love this"'. It reminds me he has a generous soul.

'Oh my God, there's the most fabulous moon over the sea,' I say.

'I can see it too, rising over the slum,' Jonathan practically screams down the phone. We are so excited to be finally sharing something.

Of course the hang-up is usually hard. Neither of us wants to do it first. We are teenagers again.

'You hang up first.'

'No, you.'

'Okay, here I go.'

'Are you still there?'

'Yes. I couldn't do it.'

And every time one of us finally cuts the line I turn into the space where Jonathan should be and I touch the emptiness.

Every day I listen to the radio news and every night I watch for him on the telly. He listens to the last hour of my program on the web. We give each other coded messages through our work. One morning I play the Faithless song 'Don't Leave'. That night, in a story he says something like, 'Colonel Patik of the Indian Army couldn't be happier about his troops' performance in Kashmir.' ('Couldn't be happier' was the phrase he'd whisper in my ear as we shared fish and chips, or met up on the dance floor of a party, or stoked the pot-belly stove at the Blue Mountains.) While these jokes convey an intimate code of love they are also laced with loss. I find his voice on the radio to be formal and removed, and my show makes him feel far away from his country. Yet we are always excited by each other's work. He is not one of those reporters who sound breathlessly excited by tragedy; his compassion seeps through his stories. This makes it easier to accept his absence. I share his success. My heart is swollen with pride.

Winter in my flat is never fun. The windows rattle and let in blasts of cold wind and sea spray, and the salt-encrusted carpet gets sodden. On still days there's a line of black haze on the horizon as Sydney lights its fires, drives its cars and makes its money. Some days the sea is glassy. At times it is roaring rough and Jonathan's pool disappears in the swell. I toast it anyway; I am celebrating the halfway point of our year apart. Six months down and six to go!

But I don't want to celebrate my birthday. Not because I still have a problem with being past thirty – in fact, this year I finally admit my age – but because I don't want to embrace rituals and mark milestones without Jonathan. He sends me an incredible bunch of flowers and calls to say all the right words, but the day drags. I realise we have now spent as much time apart as we have together and at my age – thirty-three, yes, really thirty-three – I should be in a relationship that is a little bit more settled. But it feels liberating to be honest about my age – he loves me, so I can embrace the fact that I am getting older.

Jonathan is coming home soon to cut a long story, take a holiday and go to a friend's wedding, at which I will be a bridesmaid. A few weeks before he is due to come I grow itchy with anticipation and soppy with sentiment. I revisit the Blue Mountains, the place where we spent our first weekend together. I walk over cold, bleak rock beneath silver-green gums with bases blackened by fire. Cold rain falls so its drops tickle like feathers. Boys in black beanies bog their bikes in gutters that are knee-deep in autumn leaves. This is where Jonathan grew up and I think of him as a young boy experiencing the things that helped make him the man I love. The mountains seemed warmer with him, the walks shorter, the Devonshire teas sweeter.

I send him a photo of an angel at our cemetery, praying on her knees. Even bathed in soft pink light she retains a hue of icy winter blue. He sends me a photo of our Aussie car snap on a windowsill at the Kabul Intercontinental. We look down laughing at a land where photos are illegal.

I count the hours until we meet. But when it gets to 168 (give or take an hour or two for customs) I am attacked by nerves. Will he like my new haircut? Have I put on weight? Does the real me match his memory and imagination of the constructed me? Is my life so small and superficial that he will think me mundane? When I express these fears on the phone he doesn't laugh enough. So I add: 'But at least you'll like the tattoo on my butt – your initials in a love heart.'

'What, you got a tattoo?'

We are out of kilter and our conversation is growing increasingly full of such misunderstandings. The distance is playing tricks, distorting and twisting the words he says and I mean. I ache with a need to see him.

And then five days out from the big day, India and Pakistan go to war and our plans for a reunion are the first Australian casualty. 'So selfish of them,' I joke. Again he doesn't laugh. Jonathan leaves for Kashmir and I listen to reports in which his voice grows hoarse as he competes with the sound of bombs in the background. I sprout boils of worry on my neck. Not a good look for a brides-maid.

I am also furious. Winter is a time for snuggling! Weddings are a time for appreciating the partner you have! I feel alone; my arms ache to hold Jonathan. This is the third time I have been a bridesmaid and the popular refrain I've long detested and mocked, 'Always a bridesmaid, never a bride,' goes around and around in my head.

He makes it, arriving the night before the wedding. I can't pick him up from the airport as I have a rehearsal. The bride has ordered us to perform a dance routine down the aisle, and we need to get the timing right and warn the priest of our antics. At the practice run, everyone is pink with fun, giggling with anticipation, but I feel edgy and nervous. I bolt home to find my flat empty. His flight is delayed. We've waited so long this seems unusually cruel.

And then suddenly, a car door slams and here he is bounding up my back steps. I throw open the door. He is on the mat. Grinning. He seems taller, older, younger, harder, softer, unfamiliar. We kiss with all the nervousness of the first-time pash but none of the thrill. I feel so shy and strange. The real him is slightly out of alignment with the imagined. We are out of sync. He has been in a war zone in Kashmir with Pakistani bombs echoing around him. I am amidst bridesmaid duties; fresh from a rehearsal of cackling girls and soft sentiments. He is drawn, unhealthy, slightly on edge. I know nothing of what he's been through and where he's come from, and I sense he is scared to tell me. We are plunged into false intimacy set by our own expectations and we have too much to say but no way to start. I begin gabbling and then stop myself.

I put some music on and we lie down side by side. We let our togetherness build slowly like the songs.

In the morning there is little time to talk. I am up early getting made up, dressed up and done up for the wedding. All day I am high on pre-wedding hysteria, squeezing into stomach-sucking undies, pouring the bride into her gown, scoffing champagne in the limo, reapplying lipstick. The next time I see Jonathan I am halfway down the aisle doing a pelvic-thrusting hip-rocking move to the Fat Boy Slim song 'Praise You'. He is watching intently. He looks shocked. I suddenly panic, remembering the Spice Girls night. But as I draw near I can see his almond eyes sparkling and as they meet mine he throws his head back and roars with laughter. He is laughing with me (not at me like the rest of the guests) and his laughter shows a bond that transcends distance and time. Somehow we have moved forward together while our lives have been lived so far apart.

A few days later we set off together for Alice Springs where I am to broadcast a special series of radio programs for the National Aboriginal and Islander Day of Celebration. Before the work begins we have a fort-night to holiday together. The two-week deadline on our togetherness hangs over us. I am too aware that every day will be both a celebration and a funeral, for each precious hour inches us closer to being apart. The journey into the heart of our country silences such thoughts. We have both seen Central Australia from the air – its lines of ancient mountains like the ridges on a crocodile's back, its mauve saltpans like stains of bird poo on a red table-cloth – but to be finally landing in our country's heart fills us with inexplicable joy.

Alice Springs looks like a cross between Mars and Arizona. Or how I imagine those places to be. It sits in a bowl below the MacDonnell Ranges – hills of rubble that were once mountains higher than Everest. We see the country through Jonathan's eyes. For six months he has lived in a land washed out by the swarm of civilisation. Australia is alive with technicolour, its sandy earth a bright red, its sky a brilliant bright vast blue. We are desperate to explore so we head out of town in a four-wheel drive. The ranges rear up on either side of us like spikes on a stegosaur. Sun-faded green spinifex and twisted, determined gums rise from the cracks of the crumbling range, prising the rock apart.

Ten minutes out of town we are nowhere and every-where. We feel so small below a sky that stretches forever. We camp on a huge expanse of red dirt dotted with scrub. As the sun sets, a nearby cliff turns a dusty purple and the trees a deep green; it is as if we have been transported into an Albert Namatjira painting. We sit on our esky, stare into the fire, and then let the embers warm our feet as we sleep side by side in our swag. We hear the howl of dingoes far away and are stilled by the thrill of it.

At Palm Valley we walk below giant red boulders that make us feel as though we've just entered the cartoon landscape of 'The Flintstones'. An oasis of cabbage palms sprout; relics of lusher times. Rivergums are streaked with patchy pigments of pink and brown.

At Mount Sonder we collect firewood, throw our

swag onto the ground and climb a rock to watch the sunset and drink beers. It gets cold so suddenly and so fiercely that the next day we buy the only beanies we can find at a community canteen – purple, and sporting pink Barbie dolls. First thing the following morning I am met by a romantic sight: Jonathan in his beanie, his face covered in frost, his smile huge, Barbie beaming from his forehead.

In the Finke Gorge National Park we travel along one of the oldest riverbeds in the world. It is a dry rocky track slippery with sand. As we venture further into the park the landscape transforms from dusty plains of red dirt to spinifex-dotted hills, white sandy deposits, and narrow gorges of rounded pebbles and huge boulders. There are even long abandoned cattle yards with wind-whittled posts and fallen fences. We camp at Boggy Hole – a gum-lined permanent oasis in a sea of dry. Waterhen smack the water; herons, kingfishers and crows flip down to meet them. Magnificent red cliffs rise above us. Local Arrernte people say this is where the police camped to rest after rounding up their ancestors. We can sense a haunting. In a gap in the rocks, debris from a flood shows natural violence: giant gums up-ended and thrown against each other. We don't play music in this place; the silence is a song. We don't even talk much. We bury ourselves deep in the swag. The next night the moon is so bright it keeps us awake – but it can't dim the kaleidoscope of stars. At dawn we make porridge and coffee on the fire while the waterhole awakes. The mist on the water reminds us of the swirl of sea water in the photo of Jonathan's pool.

On the road to Kings Canyon we play, stop, rewind and play an REM song over and over again. We are trying to work out the incomprehensible words to 'It's the End of the World as We Know It (and I Feel Fine)'. We argue intently about the lyrics. By the third chorus we are amidst our first big fight. For a brief moment I wish Jonathan gone. I have become used to being alone and am irritated by being challenged. Luckily we are distracted at a pit stop by a sign representing the earth's time line as the road between Perth and Sydney. The first life only appears six hundred kilometres from Sydney. The dinosaurs appear eighty kilometres from the harbour, and hominids at Circular Quay. Homo sapiens are marked two steps from the harbour. For the first time we realise our pain is insignificant. As is our argument. We doubt Michael Stipe knows all the lyrics either.

There is a photo of us from this trip that we took using the self-timer. We are upside down mid-cartwheel on the red rubble. We are careering through life together – mismatched in time, lacking in coordination, but trying the same tricky moves on stony ground while reaching (albeit upside down) for a brilliant sky.

It's an odd journey. While it's nice to be a 'we' – to share that third coffee, to reveal a thought instantly and to experience life as a couple – I feel uncomfortable for the first few days and still strangely shy. I need to rid myself of the constructed boyfriend, that imagined perfect person made all the more perfect by longing. This

happens quickly with those intimacies of camping – the
sneaking off to do the morning poo, the camp fire farts
from too much stodgy food. At first the conversation is a
little forced and veers away from things that have caused
us hurt or reveal that we have missed each other too
much. But after a week in the bush we are comfortable
enough for silence. There will be time to catch up later;
just being together is enough.

But of course there won't be time to catch up with
everything – while we have been apart we have been
growing up separately. I realise early on that India has
already changed Jonathan. At a roadhouse in Curtin
Springs he grins at the sight of big truck tyres painted
white, laid on their sides and planted with flowers. The
new Jonathan even laughs at a roadhouse sign that says:

'SEX!

'Now that we've got your attention: no shirt no
service.'

He wouldn't have cracked a smile a year ago.
Anything Australian is now beautiful to him. He has
grown so sentimental for his country he likes the Oztralia
concept! My boyfriend may have become hardened to the
follies of humanity while he was away but on this quick
visit home he needs to find faith in his homeland. I don't
challenge it.

And at Uluru I even understand it.

Of course we've seen the photos and read the descriptions of it, but the sheer brilliant beauty of that red
mound astounds us. It draws us to it. We drive towards

it laughing, and circle it close to crying. We spend a day walking around its base. By midday our necks ache and our cheeks hurt from smiling. At some places it towers above us sheer and smooth, at others it rears like a wave or dips into a hollow and then slides downward. It is stained with black watercourses and patterns that look like tyre tracks. We marvel at giant scars where blood-red stains drip down the face of the rock.

We are wrapped in the stories of the Anangu people, the traditional owners who now manage the park. The patterns on Uluru become the paw prints of the Mala or hare-wallaby. The scars morph into Kuniya the Woma python and the Liru snake she fought. We learn to spot the tracks of dingoes and goannas. We spend hours sitting under the hardy she-oaks looking out at clumps of wattle and spinifex. And on our final night we attend the sunset line-up, joining Germans in Britz campervans (we call them 'Fritz in the Britz'), tour groups in buses, blokes in utes, families in four-wheel drives and retirees in caravans. In the van beside us a teenage boy refuses to look; he sits inside, his back to the rock, strumming Nirvana songs on his guitar. We sit on the fence in our Barbie beanies eating cheese and crackers and throwing back beers. We fall in love with our country and each other all over again. Each transformation of colour on the rock – from red to crimson, from rust to orange, from purple to mauve – binds us closer. The sky breaks into bands of blue and pink, and the black bleeds through until darkness has fallen. The other tourists all leave. We can't move. We stare into the darkness, motionless. Suddenly a fat, yellow full moon rises, perfectly placed in the saddle of the rock. It lights up the land. I begin to cry. It is a Peter Allen moment!

And then we have to say goodbye again. Jonathan has to go back to Sydney to finish his story while I am staying in Alice. It infuriates me to think of him in my flat without me. But the anger is masking a sense of loss. Just when I'm used to being a 'we', to having him close, to being able to talk instead of holding on to a thought and waiting to express it later, it's over again. I fear that every time my heart cracks it gets harder to mend.

He leaves me his long distance love book and takes mine. I spend hours in bed reading his version of our months apart. How different his life is to mine yet how similar his sentiment. I cry with happiness. I think we can survive the next six months, I know we can, we have to.

A week later we are back in our different lives in different worlds. My life is organised, controlled and just as I like it. Early dawns, work, yoga, family, pubs, concerts, theatre, films, sunsets, baths. I am queen of my domain. Jonathan is again at the whim of the natural world's eruptive disasters and the violence of its humanity. He sends me a photo of our photo on an army tank that doubles as an Afghan child's climbing gym. I send him a photo of the harbour bridge at night with people on top.

We try to span our worlds by watching the same films. Jonathan sees *Shakespeare in Love*, the current hit. He rings to say a scene broke his heart. I head off to the cinema and know instantly he's talking about the scene where Gwyneth Paltrow lies with her head on Joseph Fiennes's chest – it's a simple gesture that's impossible for us.

As spring approaches and Sydney emerges from its cranky hibernation, I feel like a girl left out of the gang. There is possibility in the air, a whiff of sex on the horizon. The parties and the picnics begin. I am so sick of going out alone I stay in.

Apart is a fragile peace. Easily cracked. After being together in Central Australia, being alone is even harder. Particularly for Jonathan whose life has become so solitary; in India he is surrounded by people but no one knows him. He becomes so lonely, so tired and so over-worked he shuts down. Even from me. He doesn't want to talk on the phone, the letters trickle off. I too feel myself shutting down, growing hardened. I don't like it but I can't stop it. I feel it's futile to write in the book when he won't be able to read it for such a long time. We are approaching our limit. I am sick of the distance; he is tired of the guilt. I want to feel my face light up at his smile, his hand on the back of my neck, an intertwined ankle under a dinner table. I want to walk along the street with my hand in his back pocket. My body aches with being alone.

A decision has to be made.

I find myself keen to join Jonathan in India. I have long service leave owing – I figure if the relationship doesn't work I can come back to my job. But at the same time I feel it's time to get out of youth radio – to give the real youth, those who don't have to lie about their age, a chance. I repress my memories of how much I hated India when I went there as a young backpacker, and tell myself that I and the country will have changed. Besides, I am ripe for another offshore adventure. And for the first time in my life, I find myself open to the idea of being a kept woman. It doesn't feel like a giving-in, a cop-out or a sacrifice – it feels like a partnership. One day, I may do the same for Jonathan.

People are amazed I'm considering it. One night at a Triple J party, I'm told at least twelve times how brave I am. This makes me feel very proud of myself – and increasingly nervous. That night in bed the fears come flooding in. What if it doesn't work? I'll lose everything. I'll be humiliated. Worse, what if it does work for a while and then we break up in a few years and I blame him for the fact that I gave up everything?

The next night when I am cooking, as I toss tofu in the saucepan the oil splatters and burns my face and neck. The pain is red hot. The next morning there are huge singed splotches on my skin. I can hardly talk and have to mumble out the side of my mouth into the microphone. The breakfast comedians make jokes about the dangers of vegetarian food, but a listener who claims to be psychic rings in and says that something is telling me to stop communicating with my mouth and use other means.

I'm not sure if she's telling me to get a sex life or to

take up writing, but I need the encouragement. Doubts are still popping up when I least expect them. I decide to escape my fears by travelling to Adelaide with a friend, Jo, for a party. We return from a night of beautiful people, drinking beautiful drinks in a beautiful setting, to be met with a typed note from the hotel concierge. It reads: 'Mr Barry White called from India. He will call you back.'

'I don't get it,' says Jo as she takes the room key from my hand, which is shaking too much from laughter to unlock the door.

'It's Jonathan,' I say. 'I'm going to India,' I add.

With the decision made, I see my life for all it is: a routine that's comfortable, fun, but in some ways lacking in meaning. I want to experience the big wide world. And yet in the final weeks I mourn the small world I am about to leave behind. I mourn finishing the job I love. I mourn the view out my window. Summer is coming again. With a glass of vodka beside me, my feet on the window ledge, I watch the sky turn pink for the last few times, listen to the cicadas start their song and eavesdrop the mumble of parties. I try to hold on to every ray of clear sunshine, every soft sunset, every smell of cut grass, every swim, every tickle from the salt breeze. I have sushi each day for a week. I feel a new kind of heartache. I am breaking up with Sydney! I am breaking up with my sister and my best friend, who are both pregnant. I am breaking up with the niece I have babysat every Friday night and whom I love almost like she is my own child.

Yet while there is a break-up there is a new embrace.

Trust. For the first time I am putting a relationship first. I trust in Jonathan. This will work. My world has shifted on its axis.

As if to test my mettle the real Barry White announces tour dates. He is coming to Australia a week after I am due to depart. I don't change my flight. Friends are amazed and even I am surprised at my commitment. I've been waiting for years to see Barry but I can't wait another week to see Jonathan.

And so I leave.

It is the best decision I will ever make. Not just because I'll learn that relationships are to be nurtured not tested. Not just because Jonathan and I will outlast the Spice Girls, get married and have two wonderful kids. Not just because India will be an adventure that changes my life and who I am. But also because Barry will be a dud. It turns out he is too fat to stand up. He sings sitting with his back to the audience. He tires after a few songs and leaves the stage to the sounds of booing ex-fans demanding refunds.

Maybe some loves are better long distance.

The Lost City

JOHN BIRMINGHAM

I will live my whole life pining, just a little, for a city. How can that be? How is it that I have come to invest more feeling in a location than I have in most of the human relationships I've let fade away over the years? Her streets have never embraced me in anything but a metaphorical sense. And even then, I had to check my pockets afterwards. Her glass towers have not given me shelter from a broken heart. And to outsiders, to the jilted, the also-rans and the sloughed-off failures-to-fit-in, she looks like such a hard, calculating cynical ho that questions must be asked about my emotional balance and maturity.

How could you love someone like that, when they're so obviously wrong for you?

The city of course is Sydney. And I do love her in spite of it all.

However, I have not lived in Sydney for almost four years and I don't imagine I will again. Not for a long time anyway. I have children now, you see, and she does not care for children. She is selfish – neurotically self-obsessed to be brutal about it – and she would rather not have her absolute fabulousness ruined by hordes of shrieking little savages. They don't feature anywhere in her vision of life as it should be lived. (And the burbs just don't count. They are another country.) The city has done everything she can to make life all but impossible for her tiniest residents and their long-suffering parents. I won't go into details. I'm not here to bitch.

Instead I'm here to remember and to tell a few tales on myself. I didn't realise I was leaving Sydney as I departed that last time. My wife, Jane, had just given birth to our second child and we were booked to travel north to a wedding in Queensland. Well, that wedding fell through but we went anyway. Our families are to be found in Brisvegas, we both grew up there, and we thought it'd be nice to get away from a wet, chilly autumn for a few weeks.

We never came back.

Our house-sitters sat, rent free, in our apartment at North Bondi for nearly a year. I even maintained the cable TV and internet connections. I didn't change the phone number or any of the other utilities. I kept paying my membership dues at the RSL and carried my card with me everywhere. In case I needed to pop in for a drink. I think I was in denial.

Hell's bells, I know I was in denial.

We ended up living in Brisbane for two years, and I invested unfeasible, irrational amounts of energy in pretending that we didn't. I was the caged author at the Queensland Writers Centre. They gave me an office and in return, once a month, I gave them a couple of hours of my time to crush the hopes and dreams of embittered, unpublished writers who paid the centre for the dubious privilege of being told by me why things were likely to remain so very bitter for a long time to come.

Looking back, it was a pretty sweet gig. Sure, the 'consultancies', as we called them, were dire. But there was a bar downstairs and they knew to line me up a drink for every hope and dream I crushed on that special day each month.

Jane and I had a bizarre but amenable housing arrangement, having rented a garden apartment in an old Spanish mission block on the river directly across from the Botanic Gardens. The whole back wall of this place was made of sliding glass doors, giving us a booming view of the city, the river, and the plunging jungle-covered slopes that dropped from our back patio down to the water. A ferry was waiting just five minutes' walk away to carry me into my free office, and I think we were paying about two hundred dollars a week in rent. We got it cheap because it was eccentrically located in the car park of a hospital. Some dizzy old dear had turned up her toes and left the building to the Catholic Church, which was just waiting for the right moment to demolish it. The moment never came while we lived there.

I'd left Brisbane over a decade earlier and had returned expecting to find the same sun-baked shit hole I'd fled in search of gold and glory – but it was gone, replaced by a happier, clearly more sophisticated town. You could get fat in some of the country's best restaurants and cafés. Or find the greatest bands, the fringiest artists, the most kick-arse games designers, or the hippest architects. In fact it seemed as if a whole caravan of post-industrial would-be groovers had rolled into town while I was gone. They'd brought life to the inner city, just as they had in Sydney and Melbourne. Their straighter, richer, whiter contemporaries were building thousands of apartments in the CBD, some of them as funky as all get out, threatening to transform the heart of 'vegas into a real, living city.

It was, God help me, not completely fucked any more. And I was, like, totally elsewhere. At least in my head.

There was a café just around the corner from the lovely sandstone pile of the Metro Arts Building where the Writers Centre had me caged. I fell in with this joint because it was the closest thing to a Sydney café I could find within a comfortable distance. Indeed there were a lot of Sydney people in there every day. Some monster corporation had set up their regional headquarters in the high-rise across the street and my little café had earned a rep as the sort of place where they wouldn't spoon instant coffee into the espresso machine. (It happens. I've seen it.)

So I'd be in there every day, rubbing up hard against the sort of bizoid carnivores I'd cross the street to avoid if I was back in the ol' harbour town. The owners always had multiple copies of *The Sydney Morning Herald* hanging from the paper rack and it was my habit to read it. Cover to cover. Every day. Tuesdays were particularly exciting because the *Good Living* supplement came out, allowing me to wallow in Sydney gastro porn.

Fair enough, you might say. I still wrote for the *Herald* quite often so it was only natural that I should read the thing. But the flip side was that I flat refused to read the local rag, *The Courier-Mail*. I couldn't even bring myself to pick it up. Oh, I'd file for them every now and then. But even so, I still couldn't bear to read the thing. It would be like admitting I'd moved there or something. What little I knew of the city I was, let's face it, *living in*, I learned through the filter of another city's media; which is to say, I knew almost nothing, except for those improbable three-toed Cousin Cletus stories that were the preferred curiosities of the southern press when dealing with that strange world north of the Tweed.

There were some terrible fights over it. I had a full-contact death match with one of the arts editors from the *Courier* on local radio one afternoon. The ostensible cause of our set-to was a scabby little review she'd published by a scabby little reviewer. Not of one of my books, but of a mate's, Matt Reilly. To be fair, I had

received a touch-up from The Scab a couple of months
earlier, but of course it was published in *The Courier-
Mail*, and so I was unable to read it. Anyway, long story
short, the arts editor and I went at it hammer and tongs
in the ABC studio at Toowong while poor Steve Austin,
the host, scrambled to find some music to fill in our air
time, which was quickly filling up with vicious profani-
ties. The poxy review might have been our assassination
of Archduke Franz Ferdinand, but I think it was my
refusal to read her paper that made all-out war a
foregone conclusion.

On another occasion I traumatised a roomful of eager
young 'vegas identities at some creative industries conference when I exploded at them for wondering how they
were ever going to be as cool as those eager young Sydney
identities everyone was talking about. I wasn't really sure
what I was doing there in the first place. Actually, that's
untrue. I was there because my mate Leo was making a
motza organising this clusterfuck and he'd prevailed on
me to lend his dubious efforts a little more heft and credibility – which only goes to show how little heft and cred
there was to be had in Brisbane that afternoon. I don't
recall my exact words when the red mist came down and
my eyes rolled back to whites, but there was some table
thumping and some bad language and what I now understand was an unnecessarily violent explanation of why
they were Never Going To Make It.

It was a lot like those consultancies with the unpublished writers when I think back.

As all of the publishers, agents, editors and magazines I dealt with each day via phone and email could be found within walking distance of the Bayswater Brasserie in Kings Cross – or within cabcharge range if things got a little, uhm, shabby – it was easy to imagine that I was still in Sydney, especially when work would take me there quite regularly anyway. I probably dined and drank and bullshitted my way around Darlinghurst more often when I lived in Brisbane than when I lived in Bondi. After all, who the hell leaves Bondi?

Anyway, you're getting the picture, I guess, of a guy who really wanted to be somewhere else. You might think it odd, if you've read *Leviathan*, the huge undisciplined 'unauthorised biography' of Sydney I wrote to cash in on the Olympic Games. It is not a study in black and white, only black and the darkest shades of grey. And yet despite nearly five years of researching her greed, her misanthropy, her corruption and arrogance I couldn't help but love her all the more.

Like any forlorn suitor I can even point to the exact moment when I tipped over into the realm of lovesickness. It was well before I'd published my first book and the city had come and put her hot mouth all over me, to borrow from Michael Herr; way back in the early nineties it would have been, just after Mt Pinatubo in the Philippines erupted. That might seem a strange peg on which to hang the start of an affair, but the millions of tons of volcanic dust thrown into the atmosphere by that catastrophic eruption had a mellowing effect on Sydney.

For a couple of weeks the city was blessed with unusually beautiful sunsets.

I was walking towards Kings Cross, threading my way through the diabolical intersection at the top of William Street, when I saw my first one. It was maybe quarter to five, mid-winter, and the air was hard, cold and clear. Even under normal conditions the winter sky can act like a giant lens over the city, throwing everything into stark relief. But the blaze of colour that filled the whole world at that moment, a great fire wheel of burned orange, pale pinks and deep, rich bloody reds, lent the scenery a dramatic depth that brought me up like a snap on the reins. I found myself, with maybe a dozen others, stopping for the next fifteen minutes to watch the colour bleed out of the sky. Below us, thousands of cars crawled home along a river of light, while fluorescent tubes winked on in the high-rise towers, turning the background vista into a vast electric canyon.

It was one of the most beautiful things I have ever seen.

The natural setting of the city, the beaches, the mountains and national parks at the edge of the enormous sandstone bowl in which she lies, the 'finest harbour in the world' dotted here and there with small fairytale islands – all of these are routinely cited when discussion turns to the charms and advantages Sydney enjoys over her rivals. But rarely is the city itself, the construct of steel, cement and glass, given its due as a creation of any aesthetic worth. A bridge, an opera house, some remnant sandstone architecture, all endear themselves, but the complex, often conflicted whole isn't really thought of as being worthy of praise or poetry. Yet on this day, bathed in the weird glow of a far-off cataclysm, the city was stunning. Its lamentable concrete rent slabs, its clogged roads, its unfilled building sites, its drooping powerlines, cracked kerbing, ugly shopfronts, jammed-up traffic, lounging transvestites, scurrying worker drones and aimless slack-jawed junkies – they all took their place in a masterpiece worthy of Bosch.

Having seen a new world resolve itself around me, I couldn't wish it away when darkness fell. Increasingly, over the next few weeks I found myself fixed by new sights. A long, garbage-filled back alley, disappearing into fog. The dogleg turn in Foster Street in Surry Hills, looking like a street scene from *Sin City*, a perfect backdrop for a neo-noir encounter. A small waterfall coursing down the front steps of a strip club in the Cross during a violent cloud-burst. None of them appealing to traditional notions of the sublime, but each sublime in its own right.

And of course nothing could detract from the city's natural beauty, which might be found in the most unex-pected places, like the litter-strewn car park on the headland at North Bondi. There I discovered a small crevice in the rocks where I could shelter from the fiercest storms, while afforded a view of the bay as it seethed with white water and thundering waves.

I began to collect prints by a photographer named Caleb Carter, who specialised in capturing these rare, contrary moments, in a long study of the Harbour Bridge. Driving through, I dunno, Leichhardt, he might catch the merest glimpse of the coathanger reflected in a pool of motor oil. And he'd snap it. I sit here at my desk, in Canberra now, surrounded by his work.

A couple of years ago I grabbed at the idea of moving to Canberra because it was so much closer to Sydney than Brisbane. A mere three hundred kilometres. I told myself that given the traffic in the east I could get into the city centre quicker from the edge of Canberra than I could from Bondi, and in fact that turns out to be true, if you have to catch a bus from the beach in December. Having promised myself I'd never live in the western suburbs just to be in Sydney, I now live in the most western suburb of all, a further two hours beyond Penrith. There is a hill just outside our front door here, and if you climb to the ridgeline you'll be rewarded with an unexpected, Tolkienesque view of empty valleys and cold, dark mountains stretching away towards the Never Never.

It's odd that I should feel more comfortable here, because of its 'proximity' to my old flat in Bondi, because I suspect it was my quiet suburban childhood that gave me a fear of the burbs in the first place, a fear like in the Smashing Pumpkins song 'Muzzle', that I was ordinary just like everyone else.

Everybody likes to think themselves special, even if just a little bit. For the most part it is one of the more harmless human frailties and results in little beyond the viewing of life as a narrative in which we are the leading actors. Sydney's magic is that she understands this and whispers in our hearts that it is all right, that there is nothing wrong in seeing ourselves on a stage where we might hog all the best lines and applause. She is like LA and New York in this way. All of the things that make her so odious to decent, right-thinking folk – her obsession with glamour, her phoniness, her sometimes obscene wealth, her cynicism and lack of concern for the real proprieties as opposed to her very real concern with the mindless hair-splitting minutiae of what Alain de Botton calls status anxiety – all of these shallow vanities can make for a powerfully attractive mix.

That's right, she's bad, and who *doesn't* find that attractive?

I didn't understand her at all when I first arrived in the early nineties, although the word 'arrived' implies that I made a conscious decision to move. There was never a moment when I decided to throw over Brisbane for Sydney. I just sort of drifted back and forth between the two, until one day I'd stopped drifting. Partly that was down to my *Felafel* lifestyle choices and crippling poverty. I liked to think of myself as a bit of a jetsetter, with a home in the rainforest and another in the big smoke. I could pull off this charade because I was renting a room in my old house high up on Stuartholme in Brisbane, while sleeping on the couch at *Rolling Stone* in Surry Hills in Sydney. In Foster Street, to be exact. On the corner of the dogleg, a long time before the Swedish

Furniture Set took over and exterminated all of the winos.

I was a slow writer in those days. Max, my editor at the *Independent Monthly*, used to think that I chiselled my copy into marble slabs it took so long to file. But in fact I was just easily distracted, and kind of lazy. I couldn't afford to actually live in Sydney at that point. My first year as a full-time writer back in Brisbane I made a hundred and thirty-nine bucks – which you could live on in 'vegas, if you were moving from couch to couch, scamming the dole, and chowing down on Hare Krishna slop for two bucks a feed. But in Sydney they had guys waiting at the Greyhound terminal for people like me. Guys with big sticks to beat you on the soles of your feet for even having the cheek to show up in town with nothing but a hundred and thirty-nine bucks to your name.

So for a few months I rode the pooch between the two cities, collecting the occasional commission from magazines that didn't realise they weren't just hiring a freelancer, they were getting a new flatmate as well. I liked the couch at *Stone* because it was large and comfy and smelled of aged rock stars (think leather jackets, tobacco and stale curry farts). But the *Independent* had a full biscuit barrel and a nicer tearoom, so I often took my meals over there. No couch though. If I got stuck at the Indy after closing time it meant sleeping on a hard floor with a block of A4 for a pillow.

Why did I live like this, when people I'd graduated

with had real jobs and actual beds to sleep in? Like a lot
of young writers of that generation I'd read way too
much Hunter S. Thompson and bought into the whole
gonzo at the gates of hell fantasy. A pair of black jeans,
a three-day growth, free T-shirts and a slot on the
masthead as a contributing editor at *Rolling Stone* or,
later on, *Penthouse*. Who needs a job and a mortgage
when you've got all that?

More than that though, I had and still suffer from an
infantile need for the approval of strangers. Gore Vidal
once said that a little piece of us dies whenever somebody
we know is successful, and when I came to Sydney I was
driven in part by the corollary of this: the need for a type
of success that would, as Everclear sang, make the folks
back home scream, bitch and whine. Well, one guy in
particular.

The Coolest Man in Brisbane.

I'd met the Coolest Man in Brisbane on campus at
Queensland University, where we'd passed through the
same tutorial. He was one of those insufferable fuckers
who'd cashed in on the lottery of life. Tall, dark, and
...Sweet Jesus I can't believe I'm actually going to write
this, but, yes...handsome. He was also whip-crack
smart and ran the Coolest Nightclub in Brisbane, a joint
I'd never had reason to visit. To my way of thinking –
that is, hard up – this guy had to be getting so much
pussy that it was creating an unprecedented pussy
shortage throughout the rest of the city, with just about
every other guy in town checking their pockets and

looking down behind the cushions of the brown couch and turning around in bewildered circles right out in the middle of the street while they patted themselves down, all the time muttering, 'Damn! I'm sure I had some pussy here just a minute ago. Where did it –'

And then of course they'd see Him oozing his way up the street towards them in his snakeskin boots and reflecto sunnies and their shoulders would slump and they'd be like, 'Oh. Oh, yeah. I see. The Coolest Man in Brisbane. Yeah, sure. Sorry dude. Didn't mean to, uh...oh yeah, sure, please, take my pussy. I'm not using it. I just...'

You still with me?

So one day I'm walking through town, not really wondering where all of *my* spare pussy had got to because I didn't really have none to begin with. And still I'm ditty bopping along, feeling pretty pleased with myself in spite of this and in spite of the machine-press heat and humidity, when all of a sudden I pass into a zone of beautiful arctic chill. I look up and who should be standing there, radiating these chilled vibes, and attracting stray blondes from three blocks around, but the Coolest Man in Brisbane.

He rocks back on his Cuban heels and a smile peeks out from behind the impenetrable barrier of his mirror shades – you have to remember we're still in the eighties here.

'Hey,' he says. 'What's happening?'

'Hi!' I reply, pulling my purple stubbies just a little higher up into my armpits. 'I'm gonna be a writer!'

Well, the Coolest Man in Brisbane, who was probably on his way to his impossibly hip nightclub to have a couple of lines of top-shelf blow hoovered off his improbably long shank by half a dozen ballerinas, well, he sizes me up with his cool, calculating mirror-shade gaze. He holds it for about three seconds and then his mouth quirks in the merest intimation of a smirk and he says, 'Good luck with that,' before he slides away.

'Yeah.' I squeeze out a shit-eating grin. 'Thanks.'

I would have crumpled right there on the footpath except that down in my core there was a small cartoon character JB shaking his fist, having a *Galaxy Quest* moment, swearing that by Grabthar's Hammer he would have his revenge. But here was not the place to seek it. Here I remained in the very lair of the Coolest Man in Brisbane. To lay my vengeance on him I would first have to go somewhere his infinite reserves of local street cred counted for nothing. And that meant Sydney.

It was a private arrangement between the city and I, but no different from a million other deals she'd cut over the years. People with something to prove are always turning up in cities like Sydney, and the city's response is always the same. A raised eyebrow, a smile, but nothing so gauche and provincial as outright dismissal. She is a city of redemption and she will always let you take your best shot. After all, you might just surprise her.

She surprised me. There is a common conceit that after a city reaches a certain size it becomes an almost anti-human environment. That it is harsh and uncaring.

That natural selection is the primary organising principle, as if the metaphor of an urban jungle has become the
reality. I suspect that country folk are to blame for this
misconception. They need something to console themselves and so the myth of the heartless city has gained
currency amongst them. But they are wrong.

What I found when I first came to the harbour was a
city that couldn't care less who I knew or where I'd gone
to school. All that mattered was what I could do for her.
That might seem sadly mercenary at first blush, but
coming from a phase-locked colonial backwater such
as Brisbane was in those days, I couldn't help but be
impressed and a little enchanted. There was no hypocrisy
at work. The city wanted you to do well. Sure, if you
stumbled and fell you'd probably get ground into
hamburger meat, but that would be your own fault. You
wouldn't be excluded on general principles as would be
the case in those places where Old Money was in control.

Fucking Old Money. Let me tell you about Old
Money, mate. It's not all tweed jackets with leather elbow
patches, hunting dogs and snifters of brandy at the polo
club. A place like Brisbane, Old Money is about two generations removed from a syphilitic carpetbagger who
sold wooden dentures dug up out of paupers' graves. Old
Money was almost always stolen from someone when it
was new and a river of blood and duplicity flowed to
wash away the original sin of it. It's Old Money that gave
Old Brisbane its whole Lord Jim, legion-of-the-damned,
colonial entropy thing, where they'd insist you dress

formally for breakfast but then would not bat an eyelid if you combed your moustache dandruff into the fruit salad.

Sydney has Old Money of course, and its own power elite, which would fight as savagely as any other to maintain its privileges. But the shifting, protean nature of power in our first metropolis has meant that privilege is always immediately contingent upon circumstance and in the long run it is probably doomed. It is arguable that all the cities of the New World share this trait to some extent, but in Sydney we find it raised to the status of creation myth. The squattocracy attempted to entrench themselves here as absentee Lords, but the disconnection of their base in the hinterland from the daily life of the city made that impossible and they became an object lesson in the uncertainty of power.

That uncertainty, a recognition that nothing can be taken for granted, underlies the open nature of Sydney. There is none of the exclusivist bullshit that is often the raison d'être of smaller, dimmer, closed societies. You are a citizen of Sydney as soon as you touch down there. There is no waiting list and you won't be considered an outsider for years, if not decades, after you declare for the place. The only other Australian capital that even remotely approaches this happy hospitable state is Darwin, another city of redemption.

Naivety led me to this knowledge, but experience confirmed it. Some time in the early nineties, during my 'shuttle period' when I was regularly trailing up and down the eastern seaboard, I convinced a writin' buddy in Brisbane, Pete McAllister, that we should road trip to Sydney to score some magazine work. We were both very taken with a then new Consolidated Press publication called *HQ* (it's gone to magazine heaven now). Pete had just come into possession of a five-hundred-dollar Toyota so we pointed that thing east and drove until we hit the Pacific, then we turned right. It was winter, as I recall, and we couldn't afford to stay anywhere so we'd stop at every roadhouse along the way for the free driver-reviver instant coffee and to fill our shoes with warm air from the hand dryers in the toilets. Again, the gonzo mythology was having its evil way with us.

I don't know how we bluffed our way past the security desk in the ACP Death Star in Park Street, or even if we had to. It's possible that we just walked in off the footpath like a couple of hobos and said 'Hi, we're Pete and JB.' That was pretty much our approach when we found the *HQ* offices tucked in amongst some of Mr Packer's other fine publications like *People* and *Pix*. We'd been drawn to *HQ* because it was unlike anything we'd seen before in Australian magazine publishing. The nearest template I could think of was maybe a slimmed-down, less toney version of *Vanity Fair* in the US. They ran long, well-researched, highly polished features that you didn't see anywhere else. It was the sort of literary journalism I was obsessed with, before I became Felafel Guy. There was no good reason why we thought we could just wander into this place, stinking of two days on the road and with nothing to offer beyond 'Hi, we're Pete and JB!' But we did, and the editor, Shona Martyn, was kind enough not to call security to have us beaten on the kidneys with rubber hoses. I took my first commission off them a few weeks later. Pete became a children's book author.

I can't imagine that scene playing itself out in Melbourne, partly because there was almost no magazine industry down there, but mostly because Melbourne is not an open city. Like the club of the same name, it is a members-only affair. This isn't to run down the Victorian capital. It is a great city with a lot to feel smug about. For one thing it hasn't eaten itself alive in the way that Sydney has, thanks to some of the most rapacious property developers in the world. It has a vastly superior internal life, both intellectually and physically. Everything that happens inside happens at a much finer pitch in Melbourne, be that café life, philosophy, or doom-obsessed gothic proto-punk art movements. But Melbourne is *not* an open city.

History counts for something there, hers and yours. For instance the utterly unfathomable worship of The Footy and the messianic passions it inspires serve to deny inclusion to anyone who didn't take such madness in at the breast. Thus are the followers of the most successful teams in the AFL, the interstate franchises, barred from the magic circle of true belief. By way of contrast, Sydney, both the city and the football club, will have anyone. It can't be entirely coincidental that the Swans have opted to address their captaincy problems this year by adopting a rotation policy that could be best described as every kiddy gets a prize. It's an apt metaphor for the city's lack of investment in settled hierarchies.

As a writer who was happy to grub in on any paying gig, I found the experience at *HQ* repeated over and over again. Editors' doors were always open at least once and if they couldn't find a spot in that month's issue for you they'd help out as best they could anyway. I was once offered fifty bucks by a women's mag to pose nude, save for a Roman gladiator helmet. And when I proved incapable of turning out stories quickly enough to pay the rent, *Rolling Stone* gave me ten dollars an hour to work in the basement loading boxes onto trucks and stripping the price stickers from unsold copies of a terminally ill hippy magazine called *Simply Living*, which was published by the same house.

That was what I thought of as a sweet, sweet gig. I got to punch my ticket, because all writers need to have worked some totally demeaning shithouse McJob in their early days. And I got to hang out with Pat, the office cleaner and general dogsbody who was my first real friend in Sydney.

Patrick Bell would have been about fifty when I met him. He was a grey-haired former junkie and small-time crim who'd gone straight and somehow insinuated himself into the fringes of the rock press. The first night I slept on the couch at Foster Street, he woke me up with the vacuum as he cleaned the office the next morning. He didn't seem at all concerned to find a stranger passed out on the office sofa, and when he'd finished imposing his version of order on the chaos I asked him if he knew anywhere to get a good breakfast. He didn't, but we went anyway.

Pat pronounced his 'th' sounds as 'v's. He'd dropped out of high school but had picked up the habit of reading dense academic histories at some point. He was one of the last great jacks-of-all-trades, having taken his quids at various times from leather working, Rupert Murdoch, the breweries and petty theft. He told me he'd given the latter away after he'd been handed a flogging by celebrity bad cop Roger Rogerson. Pat and some mates had decided to turn over an RSL in the inner west. He was given the job of climbing into the roof from a convenient blind spot, from where he'd drop, panther-like, to the floor of the rissole after closing time, letting his mates in to clean the joint out. Unfortunately he had a fair load on by the time he got into the asbestos-lined crawl space, which was warm and cozy, and he promptly went to sleep, only to be woken by the elegant curses of the constabulary as they attempted to drag his drunken dead weight out of the confined hiding spot. The job, naturally, had not been green-lighted, and so they all took a fearful kicking in the watch-house at Darlinghurst.

All of this I learned, not that first morning, but

certainly by the end of the first week of our friendship. I wouldn't want you to think I was seduced by the backstage pass access I gained through my then tenuous connection to *Rolling Stone*. My first couple of years in Sydney I spent much more time boozing and bonging on with the magazine's cleaner than I did with any of the musos or pathetic celebrities who appeared in its pages. Pat had grown up in Paddington before the Great Renovation, in a workers cottage that really was a workers cottage. He told me it had no floor. You stepped through the front door and onto rammed earth. Because of his background he was able to take me into a shadow city, teaching me how to move across the inner suburbs by little used cut-throughs and back alleys he had obviously run down in his younger days, hauling a big burlap sack with a $ sign on it and the rozzers in hot pursuit. Every new hidden path and secret passage brought with it a story, which Pat enjoyed telling almost as much as I enjoyed hearing.

It was Pat who first took me over to Bondi to show me 'the big rock', a giant boulder which local legend and an official brass plaque insisted had been thrown bodily from the deep onto the rock ledge at the foot of Ben Buckler in the terrible storm of 1912. And it was Pat who introduced me to the joys of riding the Manly ferry during a storm, when a monster swell piled in through the heads and made the few minutes you were exposed to the full force of the sea an examination of just how cool you could play it.

Besides the cleaning, Pat worked the same job as me for a while, hauling boxes of magazines on and off trucks down in the loading bay, where we'd fill the hours with implausible discussions of the death of republican Rome, the idea of the individual in twelfth-century France, and the nexus between art and commerce in quattrocentro Florence, with Pat effing and blinding his way from Giovanni to Piero de Medici. We used to make great sport of the spivs and urgers who'd turn up in the loading dock with bags of stolen mobile phones and PDAs, switching from some mindless banter about the State of Origin to Pat's thesis about the importance of Greek agricultural methods to the defeat of fuckin' Xerxes at the Battle of Fuckin' Salamis and the subsequent fuckin' development of western civilisation.

He died shortly before I left Darlinghurst for Bondi in '96 and I published my next book in memory of him. It was *Leviathan*, which he was never able to read. It is dedicated 'To Pat Bell. Drinker, smoker, talker, friend. A great loss to the city.'

My first morning at Bondi I figured to get up early and go for a walk. I thought that's what people did at the beach, and I was almost right. They did get up, but it turned out that they didn't pull on crusty black jeans, Blundstone boots and a black leather jacket to take the morning air. Having lived nowhere but Darlinghurst on

the edge of the gay ghetto for nigh on seven years, it
had never occurred to me that there could be other
Sydneys.

Sure, I knew that a lot of people, most of them in fact,
lived somewhere out west, beyond the kebab shops of
Summer Hill, which was as far as I'd ever penetrated into
the mystery of the burbs, but they might as well have
been living in Perth. A revelation came with my move to
the beach – an evacuation forced on me by the end of a
long-term relationship. She got the dog and the inner city;
I got to never show my face around there again. It was
only fair, and as I said, there was a discovery thrown into
the deal. Sydney was not just one city, or maybe two. It
was a whole universe of little villages, most of which had
almost nothing to do with each other. And even within
those villages you could find smaller hamlets, occupied
by micro tribes as remote from the outside world as a
West Papuan cannibal cult. Ben Buckler, at North Bondi,
is one that springs to mind, since I eventually took up
residence there.

Here was something to be prized. Having come from a
white man's town I was aware of Sydney's compulsory
multiculturalism. But I'd never thought beyond the
obvious identity markers of race, or at a stretch, sexuality.
Everywhere in Brisbane is pretty much like everywhere
else, or rather it was. That's changed now. In those days,
however, the idea that a suburb could be a world unto
itself was still alien to me. Bondi changed that.

I lived by myself in a one-bedroom apartment in Sir

Thomas Mitchell Road, with a view into the lounge room next door occupied by the nude Russians.

The fat nude Russians.

Even so, it was all good. I'd hit the surf a couple of times a day. I had a television column for *Rolling Stone*, a bank account full of royalty payments and I had run into the Coolest Man in Brisbane while I was doing a story in Canberra, and it turned out he had morphed into a Sad Git In A Cardigan With No Nightclub Any More.

You need to imagine me doing Lleyton Hewitt's fist-pumping thing now.

Yesssssssss.

There wasn't even a karmic backlash. It just got better. I married Jane, my one true love, and when Anna was born in 2000 we all moved up to the other end of the beach, the Paris end of Bondi, and I settled into what might just turn out to be the longest pleasure cruise of my life. I had been at the beach long enough to have permanently misplaced my leather jacket, my Blunnies and all of my black jeans. I was now most often found in boardies and cheap, brightly patterned cotton shirts bought at the markets held in the playground of Bondi primary school every Sunday. I was a new man, reborn by virtue of moving a few miles to the coast. I dialled my work right back and while poor Jane was commuting into the city for work, Anna and I spent each day in a soporific routine of beach and park visits, long leisurely morning teas at Jones the Grocer, naps for everyone, and afternoon playtime. Oh, and I had cable too.

It was a *slow* life, the sort of thing being spruiked by middle-aged authors who spend a year or two in some backwater village in France or Italy to write their international bestseller. It's widely assumed that you have to move away from the city to live such a life, but I happily sank into a sunburned torpor of child care and minimal writing. Bondi, despite its tourist hordes, remains a small private world unto itself. Again, you don't need to invest thirty years there to qualify as probationary local. One winter will do it for you.

And winter is what I miss most about the place. You can still surf, with a wetsuit, but you don't have to compete with a transient population of Irish, Swedish and South American backpackers. It's mostly familiar faces out in the icy cold waves. Some you'll know to talk to, some are on a nodding acquaintance and some – like the lesbian bodyboarders at the north end – well, you'll just want to stay out of their way and never *ever* drop in on their waves.

Winter was when Jane and I would set aside three days to prepare a traditional cassoulet, the bubbling and baking stew of meats, beans and bouquet garni filling the apartment with a dense fog of wonderful smells that would bring upwards of twenty or thirty hungry freeloaders to the front door demanding to know when dinner was due. It was the slowness of the winter cassoulet that appealed to me. Nothing about it could be rushed, from the trip to Cyril's Deli to buy a dozen tins of imported goose fat, to the search for the perfect duck legs and the chopping of an acre's worth of veggies, it was a meal that demanded you give up any idea of a life outside the kitchen. For someone who got by on two-dollar Krishna slop and other people's discarded Big Macs as a baby writer, cassoulet week was confirmation that at least once upon a time I had made some good decisions. It was also an example, I guess, of what my dad once derided as the fetishisation of food, which is such an important part of contemporary urban culture in Sydney. And my dad does not use words like 'fetishisation' lightly. In fact he hardly ever uses them at all. But I think he was a bit taken aback that his two sons, who had grown up eating honest dishes like shepherd's pie, were suddenly stuffing themselves full to pussy's bow on truffled eggs.

When not gorging, or surfing or just standing on the bluff at South Bondi watching the wave trains roll in to smash themselves on the sandstone cliffs, I could often be found at the North Bondi RSL, with my face almost pressed to the glass, drinking a schooner and watching vast armadas of storm fronts moving up from the south. For a while we had a friend living nearby, a poet from the Czech Republic, and we took her down to the club for a drink one evening. There is that touching moment in the daily life of every RSL club, at six in the evening, when they light the Eternal Flame and everybody stops drinking and stands to recite the prayer.

'They shall grow not old, as we who are left grow old...'

It's quite beautiful, if a little odd at Bondi where surfers, party girls, sand punks, hard nuts, indeed everyone stands and recites the prayer to the fallen. It's such a part of the everyday ritual at any RSL that you forget how odd it must look to an outsider. Like a Czech poet for instance. The first time she saw it Dominika was absolutely floored. Her eyes teared up as she took in the sight of all of these beach bums and champion drinkers paying their respects to generations of soldiers who never got to come home to the beach. It changed her view of Australians forever. Previously she'd thought of us as a crass materialistic people. But the little ceremony with its plastic flame and awkward solemnity convinced her there was a hidden spirituality to Australian culture that had nothing to do with appropriating the original inhabitants' world view for our own. She wrote to her father about it. A veteran of the resistance against Soviet domination, he too was impressed with this quiet effort at remembrance. When Dominika left Sydney, the prayer for the fallen at North Bondi was one of the few things she took with her.

Literature and fate would both demand some balance at this point, but really, there was none. I look back now and see that even my delusional period, where I imagined myself to still be at the beach, was just a soft landing in another life. I know now that we cannot go back to Sydney, and I'm much more comfortable with that knowledge than I was when we first left. Our families are in Brisbane, where we'll soon be headed again, and many of our friends never left.

It goes without saying that there is an easier life to be had of it raising kids north of the Tweed. We'll have more space for their personalities to grow into there. The house we've bought backs onto a patch of remnant bushland, which I just know they are going to spend half of their childhood exploring. There is a magnificent tree house in New Farm Park, a short drive away, perhaps the greatest tree house in the world, where they'll probably spend the other half of their childhood. Jane and I found the coolest architect to wave a magic wand over the old Queenslander we bought. And I may yet get to lord it over the Coolest Man in Brisbane again, assuming he hasn't just disappeared into the deepest vaults of the public service in Canberra.

But that doesn't mean I won't miss my other first true love.

Because Sydney and I, we're consenting adults. I know that she only gives it up because she thinks I have something for her, but I don't care. All I ask is that she makes me feel as fantastic as she thinks herself to be – and I think we all agree, that's pretty fucking fantastic.

My feelings have not changed, but the way in which I feel them has. I love flying in to Sydney now, but even more than that I love the drive in from the airport at dusk, through the construction wasteland at Green Park, in amongst the thick, chaotic streams of traffic as they pump carcinogens into the air, turning the sunset into something that nearly recalls those few weeks after

Pinatubo. I love the looming great wall of the city's Manhattanised skyline, the promise of it, the chance that anything could happen in there. Whenever I arrive these days, I can feel the acceleration building around me as we speed towards whatever waits ahead. It feels like being drawn into an event horizon.

Great cities are about potential. Their power over us comes from the promises they make, that somewhere inside these gates, behind these high walls, a new world lies waiting to be born. New loves, new wealth, a new future spinning out from the infinite possibilities that are created when so many different paths converge in one place. A city like Sydney, which winked into existence just three lifetimes ago, carries almost none of the burden of history that weighs down, say, her mother city, London. She leaves us free to roam wherever we might, without paying heed to the accumulated woe of a hundred generations who went before. Tacky she might be. And vain. And materialistic. But she wants you to dream your wildest dreams and if you are lucky enough to see them come true she won't care where you came from or what you did before. She'll want to be your new best friend.

I miss her every day, but again as the Pumpkins tell us, some things surely have to end, and great loves will one day have to part. We had something special, the city and I. And like all great loves, we cared not a fuck for what anyone else thought. But the life I found there has led me away and we can only visit with each other every now and then.

Does she care? Not a damn.

There are always so many other suitors lined up to pay her homage. But that's okay. She deserves it.

The Heart of the Jungle

SARAH DARMODY

A monkey has stolen the Pringles. I scream extravagantly, scrabbling around beside the creaky camp bed for something to throw at the window, where not one, but two, cheeky tails are whipping back out into the dawn. I hurl a tissue box at them in vain.

'Break-in!' I yell to the Boy, who has woken bug-eyed at the sudden drama. 'How the hell . . . ?'

Little fingers have taken care to lift the latch and slide apart the mozzie screens on our rough wooden bungalow. I stumble over to the table where I laid out our food stash last night, looking with honest desperation over our diminished array of treats.

'Mint Slice!' I shriek. 'GONE!'

Out the window, the stream of colourful rubbish falling from the jungle canopy confirms the worst.

'My hot and sour soup?' I shout up into the trees. 'Come back for the beef flavour, you little bastards! No one wants the beef!'

A tail flicks. The Pringles container, unravelled in a spiral of foil and cardboard, hits the leaf litter.

'Yeah? Well how 'bout some skanky dried fruit? Oh, you didn't want that? That's still for me? Thank you. No, thaaank you!'

From the shaking leaves I hear what can only be described as cackling. A Snickers wrapper flutters down, a shiny butterfly of brown and blue. 'Oh . . . now that's just low.'

I hit my crown on the windowsill, and slump to the ground. The Boy looks on. 'Not a great start for you, Hopity, is it?' I shake my head.

'Don't worry,' he says, rolling over, 'they still have *midin* at the canteen.'

A smile blooms in my heart and reaches my face. The monkeys can keep the Pringles.

When I was eight years old, I fell in love with a curious plant. It was edible, but to describe it as a vegetable would be like calling fine chocolate a 'foodstuff'. This plant grew in an equally curious place – a country, an island, a landmass so extraordinarily beautiful and bountiful that for years after leaving I half-imagined I had made it up. Coming back now, nearly two decades later, is less like revisiting the streets and playgrounds of youth than like sleepwalking through a favourite childhood dream. The soundtrack is the same. The cries of men on the riverboats, the flutter of exotic birds, and the *nyang nyang nyang* of cheapo motorcycles slowing to a turn. The favourite, recurring, part of this dream is also the same. A wobbly chair with the sun on my hair, an orange plastic plate in front of me that is filled and refilled with *midin*, cooked hot in a blackened wok, deeply green with lush, tender fronds that curl into themselves as if sleeping. *Midin* – jungle ferns, the secret food of Borneo.

At the end of a six-month world tour involving the spending of the last of the first grown-up money we have, I begin to get nervous as the succession of jumbos we are riding move closer to the side of the planet I love the most. I'm nervous because I need it to be good there, to be warm and even half like home. We have been frozen, battered and rudely accommodated across Eastern Europe, Egypt and Northern China, and I'm looking forward to South-East Asia and Australasia, to the warmth and the people. I'm tired of old buildings and damp ruins, of palaces and dead civilisations, mean little rooms and gardens big as bath mats. I want the new, the slapdash, the ingenious, the fast-growing. My side of the world.

We trade planes in Kuala Lumpur (a gleaming city whose name means 'muddy confluence' in the language most widely used in Malaysia, a fact I find ticklish until the Boy reminds me that nobody supposes 'new castle' or 'Scott's head' to be so amusing at home). Our rattling airbus heads for Sarawak, the Malaysian half of the island of Borneo. The nerves intensify.

'The last time I took this trip was on the fifteenth of January, 1986,' I tell the Boy.

He looks at me like I'm Rain Man. 'How on Earth can you remember that?'

I'm withering: 'It was my *birthday*.'

You might imagine that at eight years old I would have been excited to have my birthday in the air, but despite a campaign to that effect run by Mum and Dad, I recall feeling pretty ripped off. No party, early presents now in the 'shipment' (a sucking black hole containing favourite items not due for months) and the general lack of focus on *moi*. I don't remember landing in Kuching, the capital city and our new home, nor my alleged room-service birthday supper at the Holiday Inn. I do remember waking in that same hotel (the only real hotel in Kuching at the time), looking out the window to the wide brown river below us, and to colourfully dressed, black-haired people riding scooters on the furthest bank. Then I threw up. I have a childhood history of doing this in new places, usually within the first few hours. Keeps everyone on their toes.

Now the plane slides down the runway from side to side like a speed skater, braking spasmodically every few seconds before disgorging us into the tropical air. The northern winter falls away like a musty coat. So pathetically pleased to be warm again, the Boy and I begin to smile and laugh, doing a crazy jangle-dance of white limbs naked to the air for the first time in months. A hot flash of nostalgia.

'Can we go to the Holiday Inn?' I ask. 'And I want to see my house, can we see my house?'

This has been going on for some hours now, and the can-we's and just-wait-till's are stacking up. My travelling companion, fresh from dragging me (sullen and unusually silent) through the frozen streets of Beijing, is managing to be patient despite jet lag.

'Sure jabber-jaw, just hang on and we'll get the bags first.'

Somewhere during the drive into town, the nerves pack up and leave for good. Twenty years later things are looking so perfect and familiar, it's like my family photo album in 3D. Even the Holiday Inn, now dwarfed by the three or four new hotels around it, remains surprisingly unchanged.

'I stayed here when I was a little girl,' I tell the desk clerk, suddenly desperate to connect with someone from this memory-place. 'We used to come here on weekends ...Do you still have the kids' menu? Goofy burger, Popeye sandwich?'

'You must have a river-view room, madam,' he tells me, in the perfect English everyone seems to speak in Malaysia. 'Let me arrange this for you, it will be the same rate.'

We pass the restaurant on the way to the elevators and an old, lost fragment blows towards me like a leaf in the air. The first morning in Kuching. I have peppermint tea in this place ('for your tummy') with Dad, while Mum takes my little brother Simon for a walk to see a peacock in a cage. 'Do we live here now Dad?'

'Yep, we move into our house very soon too.'

'Does it have a pool?'

'Mm, no, I don't think the company would pay for a pool. We can use this one, how about that?' In a jungle climate, the pebble-crete basin of the Holiday Inn pool will become our second home.

Upstairs, I am halfway through unpacking when it hits me. The fern shoots. 'Oh. My. God,' I say, and sit down. 'What?' says the Boy, 'What!' struck frozen with a face that says passports! Tickets! Fake crud from China!

'I've just remembered the best part.'

In less than ten minutes we are eating at Benson Seafood, next to the Holiday Inn on the banks of the steady river that cuts through town. *Midin* has been ordered. I slurp the salty sauce trapped by their succulent innards and crunch on their tails. After two platefuls, the sides of my tongue feel tingly, then numb. Maybe this heady, primal sensation has nothing to do with taste. It's just possible these veggies are loaded. I order another serve. I have recently learned by reading something I wasn't meant to while some real task went neglected (the way I learn everything I know and the reason I'm still not too good at anything in particular) that in addition to the four main tastes, there's a fifth, umami. Sour, bitter, salty, sweet, umami. Breast milk has it. Truffles have it. Cheese most certainly has it. A musky, intangible quality that blends deep satisfaction with moreish abandon. *Midin* must be riddled with umami.

At university, an inspiring lecturer once made our class groan orgasmically for half an hour in an attempt to explain the meaning of the French word *jouissance*, a perfect state of bliss for which the English 'ecstasy' is a poor equivalent. After more than a few warmish Carlsbergs and extra serves of *midin*, I try explaining to the Boy that I may have found my *jouissance*. 'Well,' he says with some delicacy, 'they *are* very tasty.' I'm embarrassed. They're only vegetables. Maybe it's not the food but the exclusivity of it, the fact that I can only have it here, in this place spun from childhood snapshots and now from adult appreciation. As they like to say here in Asia, 'Same same, but different.'

The tablecloth moves in and out like bellows, stirred from underneath by two cats circling hopefully around our shins. Cats (somewhat revered in Kuching, *kuching* being the Malay word for cat) are as attracted to the food at Benson as we are, and are always lurking close by. The Boy comments on the misfortune of one cat's seemingly broken tail, and I take an insider's delight in revealing that these bob-tailed cats are the genetic norm here. The cats of Kuching have fat, crooked stumps of tails that look like they have been caught in doors, some at right angles and others bent back twice – cartoon tails for turning corners. Getting drunker, I tell him that I once had a cat here too. A cat called Pynjell whose legendary marmalade coat gave rise to the metaphor 'soft as Pynjell's underbelly' which has remained the gold standard for luxurious fur in my family even after two decades and countless more household moggies.

Pynjell arrived one day in a wicker box, carrying behind him a perfectly straight tail indicating that he, like us, was an interloper in this place. He lived the life of Riley and died by the sword. After two years of luck in the jungle he was bitten by a scorpion, carried to the vet on a polished brass serving platter Mum used for Indian-themed dinner parties. I can picture the sobbing party of three in the back of a taxi – Mum and two kids crying as Pynjell moaned and shuddered, depositing pebbles of excrement behind him with each convulsion. By the time we arrived at the vet's we were hysterical and Pynjell, the Puss-cat Raja of Crookshank Road, was dead.

The Boy's eyebrows raise over his beer glass. 'A scorpion attacked your cat?'

'Mm,' I say, 'and Dad was munched on by a huge

spider that gave him a fever and left a hole in his arm where the poison went manky.'

His mouth curls up. I press on with relish.

'Simon got bitten by a painted-fly. It gave him huge boils, one even went *under* his eyelid, poor little boy. He was very brave.'

'What about you?'

I decide not to tell him about my sci-fi experience involving a twenty-centimetre ascaris worm exiting my lower intestine. The beer alone may not be enough to induce intimacy afterwards. Later, we fall asleep listening to the movement of the river and the quiet hum of the air-conditioning.

At 5.30 in the morning the wake-up call comes, and in the too-dark room I don't know where I am. A thrill rushes through me when the knowledge arrives. *Borneo.* I smile in the blackness. Fifteen minutes later finds us down near the waterfront markets, rubbing our eyes and already sweating despite the breeze and reticent dawn. The town is sleeping on around us save for a few dim lights at the furthest end of the street. We head towards them, carrying between us a camera, some water, and the worst-smelling bug repellent I have ever encountered. This is the time of day I refer to as the 'mission hour', the time I never see unless it involves some kind of grave purpose or improbable destination. Or pancakes.

'Don't orang-utans ever want to sleep in?' I ask, yawning with most of my face.

'Dunno,' the Boy says. 'They make nests in trees overnight. Maybe some are better at it than others.'

Cheaping-out on a guided tour, we are catching the only public bus to Semenggok, the Orang-utan Rehabilitation Centre, that will coincide with the orangs' breakfast-time.

Our own breakfast comes from a tin-roofed shack by the river, where a smiling man wipes his hands on an apron and ushers us inside. 'Coffee?' he asks. It comes quickly and is strong, sweet, made with Nescafé and condensed milk. '*Roti cani*?' Blank. He tries again. '*Ro-tea chan-eye*.' We are lost until the chef points to something familiar. It's a flaky, fried flatbread much like pastry, a good breakfast treat.

'Yes please!'

'Can cook with egg,' he offers. 'Very good, pree-mium!' He's right.

Our bus arrives and then shudders off into the softly rising light. We slide on sweaty legs across the vinyl seats, smiling from a coffee buzz and the promise of a wildlife encounter.

'Creatures!' I say.

'I know,' the Boy agrees, 'I know.' Our fingers interlace despite the heat.

The view is lush and welcoming. Smiling faces, tidy houses, creeping vines. 'Hello!' people wave, 'Hello!' and for the first time since we left home it's not the 'Hello missus' that ends with 'buy my picture/camel ride/Great Wall/pyramid/cheap pasta/best price/I give you.'

'I like this place,' the Boy says.

'Me too,' I say. 'Me. Too.'

Off the bus, we walk a kilometre down a jungle path. Butterflies as big as my hands are riding invisible currents, and exotic, carnivorous pitcher plants (so named for their water-jug shape that traps food and fluid) are dangling out of trees and around our feet. At the park's entrance, the ranger greets us.

'Hello! Good morning! I hope you will see Richie today!'

'Who's Richie?' we ask.

He points to a mounted photograph. The animal pictured is enormous, a giant golden man with a massive, swollen brow and fur the colour of burnt sugar-threads.

'That is Richie, King of the Jungle.' The ranger contemplates the King. 'But sometimes he sleeps in.'

He tells us we have arrived during a bountiful fruit season, and the orang-utan population often skips breakfast in favour of their own foraging.

'What do you feed them?' the Boy asks.

'Mm, we start with some good bread, some milk, a few eggs, and then fresh fruit too.' The Boy looks longingly into the trees. He nudges me. 'Can I move in?' he whispers. 'I reckon that sounds pretty good.'

At breakfast-time, we follow the ranger through the trees and wait at a distance. He motions for silence, and then calls. It is an eerie noise, the kind that prickles at your neck. A lonely sound that wanders and disappears. We wait. In the quiet of the jungle, the significance of this trip begins to sink in. Where I am. How far we've come. How much I've missed it here. My eyes suddenly fill and I pray for Richie to appear quickly. The ranger calls for half an hour. Then he shrugs. Richie must have found a good nest-maker to shack up with.

The Boy sees my crumpled face. As we walk to the bus stop, he does a leaping, screeching chimpanzee for me.

'Hey, don' worry mon,' he says, sending in his reggae alter ego, 'mon-key doin' his best, he got no 'larm clock, he no commuter, he don' dig da nine-to-five.' I smile, but a little bean of something has crept in during the quiet, and I can feel it germinating between my ribs. I don't want to know what it is.

Back in Kuching, I show off every corner of the little city as if I founded the place myself. I point out the proud white building on the far bank of the river. 'Check it out,' I say, 'Fort Margherita.'

The fort sits high on a grassy hill across the water. On our side of the river, the Boy finds a newly set plaque explaining the view. 'Raja Brooke,' he reads, 'the white Raja of Borneo, built Fort Margherita and named it for his wife. Now it's the Police Museum.'

'Oh yeah,' I try, 'Brooke was British? A colonialist, right?'

'Mm, he seems to have won Kuching on his own though. Says here he was a privateer and explorer; he chased off some pirates and the grateful Sultan of Brunei gave him this city and a chunk of Sarawak. The Brooke family dynasty lasted a hundred years from 1841 to the Japanese occupation.'

'I knew that,' I say, 'sort of.'

The information is slipping away from me. It occurs to me that I never studied the history of this place while at school here in Kuching. I grin. I didn't study much of anything. There was too much other nonsense afoot.

In the beginning, our new school felt like Hogwarts. Due to the collision of numerous religions and languages, everything was topsy-turvy and, for my six-year-old brother and me, deliciously odd and chaotic. Our class-mates ate salty fish porridge for breakfast (eye of newt!) while others would often have to fast for weeks, taking nothing but water from the bubbler during the school day, regaling us with tales of midnight family feasting (the witching hour!). Some were deathly afraid of pork, reacting to packaged salami sticks as if they were kryptonite, while others happily confessed to eating crisped-up trotters and piggy snouts as if they were special treats. We could never tell when one of our innocuous English words would be greeted with hoots, having translated into something to do with bottoms or the smells they make. I discovered magic of my own. One day our class did an exercise on 'hair', each of us writing down three common properties of hair. This calls for more contemplation than you might think. I put 'changes colour when wet' in at number two. My Chinese teacher led the children in much laughter at my expense, until I dipped my long blonde ponytail in the fish tank, just to prove the point. When it darkened they gasped as if I'd calmly removed my teeth.

I resume our haphazard tour through Kuching's charming streets. The sun is shining down on the city's many parks and courtyards, giving life to the riot of plants that are stretching out in all directions and colours, sometimes threatening to push apart the walls of old buildings through fist-sized cracks. New buildings have gone up – ubiquitous Asian shopping towers in glass and gleaming tiles – but they seem to have settled in nicely beside their older neighbours. The riverfront has been tastefully redeveloped since I was a child. Muddy gravel has been paved over with bricks and planter boxes, but much else is the same. On weekends and holidays, this is where I used to wait with Dad and Simon for tiny, leaky boats to arrive. Back then, it was my job to hold the coins for our fare, Dad's to talk to the river-men who used curved knives on the coconuts we bought for snacks, and Simon's to check for pirates as we sailed the four-and-a-half minutes to Fort Margherita on an 'adventure!'. Mum would be waiting across the street when we returned, after a round of tea and gloopy local sweets with her artisan friends, laughing in two languages in the back rooms of their galleries. If happiness was a place for me, it was here.

After an hour of wandering, the Boy is smiling too. We stop by the Sarawak tourist office and literally buy the posters off their walls. They are clever and beautiful, modelled on paperback covers for adventure stories of the thirties and forties. 'The Leopard Sang in Borneo' reads one, 'The Lost Idols of Sarawak' another. We go to Ting & Ting supermarket, the little shop that could. Mum and Dad always bought things from home here, from 'Oz' as the owner used to say, and the new century has improved the inventory. The Boy and I have been away from home for many long months and the few Aussie things for sale excite us. 'Bega cheese!' I shout. 'Pizza shapes!' We buy Twisties and the ill-fated Mint Slice biscuits. On the way back to the hotel, we pass a Chinese temple in the middle of town. The Year of the Rooster is only a week away, and the brightly painted temple is strung with necklaces of lanterns, printed with characters promising luck and fortune.

'Si and I used to light incense sticks here,' I recall aloud, 'and sometimes we burnt paper money too. It was great, playing with fire and the destruction of grown-up property. Two naughty thrills in one.' I am downplaying it. The awe we felt, the responsibility to those strange smoke-hungry gods. The Chinese feature heavily in my memories of the technically Islamic Malay city of Kuching. Apart from their wonderful food, I remember the pageantry of Chinese life. Dragon dances and ropes of firecrackers, red money packets and sweet cakes handed out at New Year's. On the way home from school we used to pass the colourful ceramic headstones of the Chinese cemetery in Kuching, and our friends would urgently instruct us to 'Hide your thumbs! Always hide your thumbs or the dead can find you!'

All the local gods and superstitions had truck with us here. I figured you never could be too sure. Mum did yoga with an Indian neighbour whose lounge room featured shrines to many-armed and elephant-headed gods. Some were blue. I liked them. The Hindus in Kuching held the festival of Deepavali every year; we watched as men in trances pierced their tongues, backs, and other flesh with skewers and fishhooks weighted with oranges.

After a quick snack of satay outside the mosque, I insist on visiting the Kuching museum so that the Boy can have a break from my rambling 'when I was a girl' soliloquies and be a traveller again rather than my sounding board. It is hot too, enervating and sticky, and I'm looking forward to some air-conditioning. Upstairs in the old building is a re-creation of a room from a longhouse. These large wooden structures are built high above the jungle floor on stilts, home to entire communities of the indigenous tribes, the original 'headhunters' of Borneo. When I was small, these people fascinated me most out of all the weird and wonderful grown-ups and goings-on of Kuching. I remember peeking at night-dances of Iban men, adorned with feathers and ornately carved shields, the prized beaks of hornbill birds in their headdresses. When Dad, a water treatment engineer, had to travel to the remote dam site of Batang Ai, we went with him to visit the longhouses there.

In the museum, I am a good girl for about five minutes, before I'm unable to contain my excitement and begin chattering away again. We saw, I tell the Boy, human skulls strung up with rattan, and had been ordered by Mum (on threat of silent pinching) to treat this as normal and perfectly respectable. We had nodded to the grouped skulls as if they were daisies. Oh, love what you've done with those Japanese ones, isn't that clever! Nice work with those betel-nut spittoons, we smiled, we spit red all the time at our house too.

Many tribespeople had adapted to the comparative city life of Kuching, and they still seemed to hold some cultural power here. Their artwork was especially revered, and many of their languages and customs were also preserved, gleefully mangled by Simon and I during impromptu performances for Mum and Dad. Other local symbols were incorporated into our dreams and our play. The ornamental *Kris* knife took the place of fantasy daggers in our games; Muslim hats, carried mats, and the daily call to prayer could be interpreted as the calling cards of a dangerous, secret society if one had read too much Sherlock Holmes and wanted to scare one's brother. We ate bat, I tell the Boy, shark's fin, whole soft crabs and small crustaceans called 'bamboo worms.' Unripened coconut juice, black soy-bean drinks, and gelatinous Chinese desserts that looked like fluoro green spaghetti.

'What was your favourite thing?' he asks, 'Apart from the *midin*?'

I search. 'Ovaltine,' I say. 'The other kids drank Milo, but we knew what was what.'

Back at the hotel, the Holiday Inn pool is a great deal smaller than I remember, joining the list – along with high schools, bedrooms, park swings and summer campsites – of things-that-shrink-with-years. Slipping into the too-warm water, I have a vision of lounging in the shallow end watching a German girl with her boyfriend. I was nearly ten by then, and I knew nothing about boyfriends. After two years here, I hardly knew any boys. In the hotel bookstore there was a Judy Blume book called *Letters to Judy*. I used to sneak in there and read it with wet hair trickling water to my feet, hiding behind the shelves hoping not to get busted. It became my manual for the outside world, the world with boys in it, along with old copies of *Cleo* and *Cosmo*. I close my eyes and float. I can still feel the confusion, lying on my wooden bed under the ceiling fan, the jungle thick with noise and smells outside my window, while I read odd sentences about chlamydia, good handbags, crafting the perfect résumé, and nipple discharge. The longer we spent here, the more my imagination improved. My quest for the world beyond Kuching slowly became insatiable.

'You didn't even have TV, right?' the Boy asks, ordering drinks and politely half-listening. We are lazy with the humidity. Our bodies are still adjusting to breathing soup and the shock of yet another time zone. The light too. The glorious equatorial light after so long in the troglodyte gloom.

'We had a little,' I say, 'but it was almost worse than none.'

An hour of English-language programming ran every night on local TV. Simon and I would go into our Amah's room to watch it on the household box. Our Amah was from a village, or *kampung*, outside town. She lived with us during the weekdays, as far as we could tell, to scramble eggs, iron Dad's shirts and wash the floors with Mum. It was strange at first, but everyone had an Amah, and she became kind of like a neighbour and exchange student in one. She watched the TV shows with us to improve her English, and we sat on the end of her bed while she played with our hair.

The programs were interrupted frequently and in random places by a series of loud Malaysian commercials. Our favourites were the ads against '*DADAH*!' Years later I would find out that *Dadah* means Drugs (drugs with a capital D, as in capital punishment). The ads featured booming voices, fake blood and dramatic music, and invariably ended with a swinging noose. They were the original Itchy and Scratchy. We loved them. Simon and I would laugh and make fake strangle-faces, each pretending to have died the nastiest death in order to gain our Amah's attention. '*DADAH*!' we cried to each other, '*Tidak DADAH*!' and played the dead-as-*Dadah* game while Barlow and Chambers were

imprisoned in mainland Malaysia, awaiting their real
deaths. We were ignorant of our doomed countrymen as
we aped the commercials between 'Magnum PI', the
'Golden Girls', 'Family Ties', and 'Leave it to Beaver'. As
months and then years passed, these shows became how
we connected with western culture.

'It's a wonder we didn't end up in prison ourselves,' I say,
'with all that bloodthirsty, subliminal education instead of
the Smurfs.'

Merely teased by the occasional story-line involving
Alyssa Milano on 'Who's the Boss?' my growing fascina-
tion with teenage life wasn't being satisfied by television.
We made friends with an Australian couple in town who
worked for a battery company. When they returned from
an annual trip home I peppered them with questions.

'For example,' (I often started sentences this way – it
always seemed professional) 'what music do teenagers
listen to in Australia?' They told me it was the Hoodoo
Gurus and INXS. I looked for pirated tapes in the
markets for weeks and came up with Madonna instead.
Madonna is everywhere. 'Material Girl' will be the
soundtrack of the apocalypse. Someone at the British
consul donated me a *Smash Hits* magazine. There was a
poster in the middle of Billy Idol. I took it out, put it on
the wall and covered it with lipstick kisses (Mum's good
Guerlain, sorry Ma), just as I had gathered you were
supposed to. Idol's snarling face frightened me, and I
didn't understand his spooky music, but I persisted.

The Boy finds this hilarious. 'No wonder I like Spike

on "Buffy",' I muse, 'I was conditioned.' We are getting a little drunk in the sun, helped along by the early morning start and the diesel fumes from the river traffic beside us.

The Boy has been quiet, recovering from a few hard months of being on the road. It's just been the two of us for so long now. We've worn out our stories a bit and recycled some bad jokes. This is also the first stop we've made where only one of us is a stranger, and I'm conscious of squashing the joy of discovery. I ask the Boy if he wants to explore on his own awhile, but it's the selfish 'Are you sure you don't want that?' type of question which just means 'Sorry.' I need to share this with someone, but I feel like I've invited him to some kind of reunion only to wander off into corners without him.

'What do you want for lunch?' I ask, by way of compensation. The Boy rubs his hands together. 'Ben-SON!' he replies, and we make our way through the hotel car park to a corrugated iron wall beside it, with a hole for a door and a point-to seafood menu on ice.

After another lunch consisting largely of *midin*, we travel to the food markets on Jalan Satok. We see a startling array of meats, fruit and vegetables, as well as several subtle varieties of *midin*. None of them look like the decorative and native ferns we have at home in Australia, and I'm not even sure what to ask for when I get back there. I consider taking a sample and asking for a horticulturist to meet me at customs. I consider paying

the fine. I consider jail time. I pick up a bunch and vacil-
late. 'No.' The Boy is right, but I'm sorely tempted.

A familiar smell is coming from some large, bulging
hessian bags standing upright near strips of hanging
jerky. They are filled with different kinds of dried and
salted fish. These were another favourite snack of mine. I
remember going to the old Kuching cinema one rainy day
and taking a bag of them along with me. A visiting family
friend laughed at me. She told Dad he wouldn't need a
stick for beating the boys off if I was going to take salty,
pongy fish to the movies. I can still feel the shame of
picking the *wrong movie snack* – what an imbecile, what
a rookie. I longed, with all the zeal of an anthropologist,
for a group of kids to study and set me straight on these
matters.

I only saw two movies in the two-and-a-half years of
our life in Kuching, the only ones in English that made it
to us, (probably a year or so later than everywhere else) –
Labyrinth, starring muppet creatures, and *The Living
Daylights*, starring 007. I think I saw those two movies a
hundred times over, stunned each time by the drama, the
colour and the fantastical adventures made possible in
the world of the screen. I fell in love with the cinema here.
There was plenty of time to fall in love in the jungle, even
if you didn't know any boys. The weather was warm, the
days were long, life was easy and no one worried what
you were up to. With one new movie a year and limited
TV, reading became my first love, my first adult passion.
My first 'hobby' that didn't involve sugar or Mattel. A

woman whose children were away at boarding school would give me boxes of her kids' books when they returned for each new semester. The kids were older than me, teenagers already, so I was immediately interested in anything they were interested in. I devoured all the books without prejudice, and fell deeply in love with the printed word.

Photographs of me at this time show a pale girl, tall for her age, with gangly limbs draped over furniture, a book always gripped in her hands. Thin cotton dresses to fight the heat, books growing thicker to combat a lust for knowledge of grown-up life, of love affairs, of transformations, of entry into that place where Alyssa Milano hung out, where I had decided I would need to know about jeans, velvet hats and holding hands. My complex fantasies had once involved fairies, dragons (good and bad), winged horses and secret houses in the woods. These played out easily in the jungle. Once they began including Princes Valiant, Chivalry and Charming, first kisses and rescue from danger, I was forced inside, full-time, searching through my books for satisfaction.

Today, this love affair is getting me into trouble. It is a new day. A hot day. We have taken a boat to Bako National Park, an hour outside Kuching. The Boy has just carried my heavy bag through a hundred metres of sucking swamp, only to discover it has six books in it.

'Hoppy, what are you doing?' he demands, greasy grey mud up to his calves. 'We're only here for three nights, are you going to read all day?'

'You brought stuff too!' I say. 'All that food and your leech socks and whatever . . . oh, look, a wild boar!' and thankfully, it is one, a mammoth tusked creature that truly looks like something from the *Labyrinth*. Which must make this the Bog of Eternal Stench. I lose a thong down deep in the muck, searching for it with my foot for too long, unwilling to get my arm covered in what feels like poo and looks like wet cement. Mudskippers keep popping up as my audience, standing erect on slimy tails, their comical little eyes blinking.

The Boy reaches our hut first and drags the gear inside. He strips off his sodden T-shirt and hangs it on the rail outside. He looks at me, smiling, as he does this. It is a perfect white smile with deep dimples, and the body revealed by the absence of T-shirt is tall and brown and strong. Gorgeous in the way of youth and the lack of vanity. It suddenly strikes me. All the reading and dreaming of princes I did in this place, and now I have one. I have my grown-up love at last, but instead of dragging a smile to my lips, this thought causes the troublesome bean inside to grow again, without warning, wrapping its tendrils tighter. The complications of adult life don't have all the glamour and freedom I once imagined they did. Childhood had that. Hours in our overgrown garden while our imaginations ran wild and we forgot time. Jungle insects and animals to poke at and contemplate, Simon climbing with noisy macaque monkeys who ripped his pocket off looking for food. When Nan came to visit they stole a roll of antacids right out of her bag. The glow-flies at night, the undulations of centipedes as thick and long as snakes, the grooved scales of a dead pangolin that Mum dried and made into a necklace. Out of the hard knotted grass and the clay soil, Simon and I would make castles and dream aloud for hours.

'I am back in time,' I tell the Boy, 'Want to hear what it's like?'

'Go ahead,' he says, indulgent while the beer is still cold.

I learn to cook here in Kuching. I make 'diabetic specials' for Simon, whose pancreas had decided on a go-slow at the age of four. These gourmet creations involve the cooking up of calorie-free food including celery, cucumbers, zucchini and dill pickles (our favourites), all fried in extra pickle juice in a pan. Sometimes I put flour and water together to roll out 'snakes' of dough. I curl them into small shapes and watch as they dry hard on sunny tiles. They are disgusting, but the process has the right degree of chef-like importance. One day I cut up Mum's lemongrass plant and brew tea from it. This pleases me. I am a farmer.

The Boy laughs. He can see me here. He sighs for me. 'You must have had quite a tantrum going home to Oz,' he says.

'I actually couldn't wait to leave,' I say, and surprise myself with the truth.

'I don't believe you.'

'Mm. Neither could my parents.'

Life in the jungle is a fairytale for us, I continue, a hyper-reality. So it is a surprise when I begin to cry and beg and wail to return to Australia. A yearning I don't really understand, and neither must Mum and Dad, who imagine I know little of the country we come from. They know the suburban life we will return to; I do not. My dreams are simple. I imagine orderly suburbs filled with kids like me, and with teenagers too, teenagers and their exciting lives. There will be carpet on the floor instead of tiles, cats who stay inside unmolested by ridiculous, extravagant wildlife like scorpions and jungle vipers. I long for cartoons on TV, for the kinds of grocery stores on the English-language sitcoms, for unpowdered milk, for picture-book streets without cavernous, open storm drains, and even for seasons, for mittens and sneakers. I long for the First World. My Barbies live in the jungle, but those tarts want the city life. Their plastic cars zoom through thick ferns and around the roots of banyan trees. They want out. They want Ken.

Dad makes it worse. He brings us frozen meat pies home from a trip to Oz. A huge fuss is made over them. They taste like Australia, the Australia I know that is my smiling grandparents, hot golden beach-sand at Christmas, the road burning my feet as we run to get icy poles, potato scallops, fried fish and (yum) pies. Mum offers a pie to our Amah, who giggles and covers her mouth. She thinks our food is funny, and won't listen when Simon begs her not to put salt all over slices of Granny Smith apples.

I tell the Boy a fraction of everything that was. We are lying beside each other now on the white shores at Bako, still the most perfect beach I've ever known. We are picking the remains of a coconut from our teeth. It washed up like a special delivery, and we smashed it high up on the rocks, away from the sand.

'You must have been a funny little thing.'

'Aren't we all?'

And we are. Tweenagers, little half-people playing with dolls and dreaming of adult life, desperate to learn the rules of the ungovernable world.

The Boy rolls onto his back and luxuriates in the sun. 'You must have missed this though,' he says. 'It's like Tarzan out here.'

Of course I did.

We go home to Oz, and the First World is not the clean and homogenous sitcom I believed it would be. We have a new Jungle here, the Bush, where tarantula-like huntsmen creep into my room through wall vents, snakes hide in grasses at midday, shoes have to be shaken out, and gardening gloves are death traps. Spiders with fat red bums hide in bricks and the wood bin, and will kill you. The rain comes and is not warm, nor is it stopping. It's the great wet of '88. I walk to school, another young-adult literature dream of mine, but the path is cold and muddy, and goes right through that spooky Bush again. Magpies swoop at me, and orb weavers build enormous nests, from which they hang as big and hard as small crabs.

Mum is misty-eyed over our new school. It is set on a huge expanse of playing fields and ovals, clapboard demountables on stilts surrounded by gums. She says it reminds her of her childhood, her coastal Australian country school. I am disappointed. I wanted a big red-brick school like on telly. The grass is disappointing too. 'Oh, Kuching grass!' I say, dismayed, longing for delicate soft ribbons that grow for children's feet in movies, the grass of Enid Blyton I had imagined would be here, in the real world. This Sydney grass is thick, waxy and knotty instead. The same tough stuff I'm used to. Dad tells me it's because even though Australian soil is very different, it is shallow like Kuching. The nutrient is only a small layer in Australia, the rest is dry and hard.

In Borneo, school lunches had consisted of *kway teow* wrapped in greased newspaper, delivered by an old woman with a gray-haired bun, two teeth, and no English. I loved it. Now there's a new kind of tuckshop. Mum joins with the other kids' mums in serving pies, sausage rolls, salad sangas and lamingtons. Thankfully, I love them also, and anyway, I'm now too conscious that my old lunches would be embarrassing here. The smells and the wrapping. My new classmates would laugh at old Mrs Ng and her stained, trembling hands. We join 'houses' at school, named Wombats, Wallabies, Koalas and Emus. I'm a Wombat. It's a different kind of Hogwarts. We learn history at this school and I like that.

We learn the history of our country and, despite muddled accents, we begin to feel a part of that history. We are migrants, my brother and I, migrants from the jungle, but we are blonde and Skippy, so the only club we can safely feel our difference in is the club of two, of each other.

The constant rain pounds the earth in front of our house. One day enough of it has washed away that it exposes the knotted roots, which form tiny caverns and platforms like the ones we used to make our fantasy fairy-houses in Borneo. We go outside and play for an hour or so, but it's not the same. The lure of the television calls us in, and besides, we would die if our friends saw us, our new friends who play games like netball and cricket, games we've barely heard of. We are used to playing in the mud and vegetation with our hands and our heads. This same night our new socks are drying in front of the gas heater. Wind whips through cracks in our damp old house under renovation, and we are slack-jawed in front of the telly.

An ad for Malaysia comes on. I can feel the light on my face, hear the birds and smell the briny pools at Bako beach. I can taste *midin*. We look at each other with shining eyes. We didn't dream it, it's real, it's out there still and now it's in here, it's found its way to us. 'Mum,' we yell, 'Muum, Malaysia's on telly!' She rushes in and we all smile and grin, like it was our own house on the screen, like we could see ourselves, happy in the jungle, waving back.

I tell the Boy all of this, trying it out on him to see if it makes sense. We walk back through the jungle as I talk, back to our hut. By the end of the story I am crying. The bean has exploded with growth. I cry for an hour, a world-class snit. Tears pouring out of my nose, eyes swelling shut. I rub mozzie repellent into them and make it worse. 'What is it?' he holds me, and now guilt creeps in too, for ruining our night in the jungle, for letting the past push the present so far out of the way. 'Shh,' he says, 'what's wrong?'

'It's still here but it's all gone,' I tell him. 'I wish Borneo had fallen into the sea.' The more I remember the more I know I've lost. I must have forgotten to put my thumbs down; I'm being chased by ghosts. The people in my memories are gone. The little boy who was my brother is six feet tall and a man of his own. He cooks for himself now. The laughing sweethearts who were my parents, the island that was their bed on Sunday mornings, are lost to me. They live with oceans between them, their beds are shared with other people and cannot be my hiding places. The mysteries that consumed me then have been solved – teenage life, correct movie snacks, the love of boys, then men, even *Dadah* and death. I cry harder, feeling old for the first time, used up, unable to regain the clear-eyed innocence I felt in this place, the pure wonder for the world and all the things in it. 'That happens to everyone,' says the Boy, then, clutching at straws, 'but new things come.'

'It's not as good,' I insist, it can never be as beautiful

as when you don't know it all, when you just have to imagine the rest. I sob, dehydrated and unlovely, too hot, bothered by insects. 'I thought this was a place,' I cry, 'a perfect place, but it was a time-place. And so nothing in it can come back to me now.'

He rocks me. It goes on. Finally, he asks, '*Midin*? Still the same. Still pretty good, eh? And you showed me. I never knew about it before. Or Sarawak Chicken Rice, or *murtabak*. Now I have it too.'

It's just enough for me to sleep on. I sleep deeply, despite the heat. Outside our thin walls monkeys are sleeping too – the children, grandchildren, of the same monkeys who used to steal Mum's sunnies, Simon's jelly beans, Dad's hat. The monkeys will wake at dawn, and in the first light, there will be a break-in.

Heartache

Adapted from *The Colour of Panic*,
a play by Nicholas Hope.

NICHOLAS HOPE

By December I was drinking up to two bottles of wine a
day. Cheap wine by Norwegian standards, expensive by
Australian. I was running out of money but there didn't
seem much else to do. The world was easier through a
haze. Other people were skiing or walking in the forest
or whatever they do in winter in Norway. If I complained
about boredom or feeling down they'd say: 'You should
ski or go for a walk in the forest.' But I can't ski and it's
freezing out there in the forest and anyway once you've
finished skiing or walking what then? The world is still
there and it hasn't changed while you were out. So there
I was one night, on my second bottle of wine – maybe it
was day, it's hard to tell, it's just as dark either way –

when my girlfriend broke a two-week silence and said: 'I've got this video, let's go upstairs and watch it,' and I thought about it and said: 'I can't go upstairs, I think I'm having a heart attack.'

Now I'd been noticing my heartbeat for some time but I hadn't mentioned it. The last few weeks the heart had been going pretty fast and it was tiring but I understood I wasn't much fun to be round, mooching in the chair getting slowly drunk and complaining all the time, so I hadn't wanted to mention anything. I was trying to be good by being silent. Besides, maybe it was just the wine and once I stopped drinking so much the heart would slow down or something. Or maybe the skiing walking bug would descend on me and I'd get healthy. But the more I thought about it and thought about the symptoms, especially this night, the more I thought the situation was critical.

And it was. My heart when my pulse was taken was going at a hundred and eighty beats a minute, my arms felt like little needles were extending all the way down to the palms, my limbs felt like lead weights, I couldn't even lift the glass to my lips any more. And that was a major loss. I wanted to tell my girlfriend whose country this was, 'See what this place has done to me?' But how could I? She could see it anyway and there she was sleeping on the floor beside the hospital bed. It would have been churlish to rub her nose in it, she'd nearly started crying as she translated the symptoms to the doctors. She thought I was going to die and it made her sad. I could hardly say: It's your fault for being Norwegian.

The doctors thought I had an infarct. It sounds like something from fundamentalist Islam but it's a blockage in an artery. The drugs they'd given me to slow my heart down had no effect. The only explanation they could think of was an infarct. They sent a tube through one of my arteries that injected dye into my bloodstream as it went, and we all watched it travel via X-ray. I could feel it too, this warm sensation all through the body, a bit like when you piss yourself. 'That,' the doctors told me via my girlfriend, 'is the heart reacting to the tube in the veins, it's a kind of rush like drugs but it can end up giving you the heart attack we're trying to prevent. If it gets painful or you think you're going to pass out, tell us.' We all looked really hard at the X-ray screen and everything was normal. Not that I could tell, I was just fascinated by looking inside myself, watching the grey dye spurt in time to the heart, just a millisecond after each beat. That's me in there, I thought, that's my mechanics, that's what's keeping me going, one day that will stop and so will I. I couldn't tell if what I could see was normal, but the doctors said it was. There was no infarct, there was nothing abnormal. Just a super-fast heart. After four days they told me I could run a marathon so far as they could tell, there was nothing wrong with me, my heart would slow down soon, it was already down to a hundred and twenty beats a minute. I was free to leave the hospital. I should just relax and I'd be fine.

They told my girlfriend and she came to collect me. She was pleased I hadn't died. She waited happily for me to get ready. I put my lead-weight arms into my lead-weight singlet, then into my lead-weight shirt, pullover, overcoat; my lead-weight legs into my lead-weight underpants, leggings, jeans; my lead-weight feet into socks, more socks, wet-weather boots; my slow-motion head into a woollen beanie; my slow-mo neck into a woollen scarf. I walked out into the winter grey, and my heart jumped back to a hundred and eighty beats a minute, and I wondered: What is wrong with me?

Grey! came the answer, in a clipped voice hissing inside my depressingly sober head. *Grey is what is wrong with you. It's grey outside and now they've pumped grey inside as well. They're turning you grey.*

'It's true!' I thought, pulling and pushing my laden body towards my girlfriend's borrowed car in the middle of the snow turned sludge, my heart peaking in the attempt to pump colour into my life. 'I never knew what panic and claustrophobia were until this first winter. Everything *every*thing *everything* closing in, a losing battle. No wonder I've been drinking!'

My girlfriend strode ahead. 'I'll start the car,' she said. I peered round, newly enlightened. Light seeping. Sun so low that when it *does* appear it's insipid, a hint of warmth and light on a far, other blessed horizon. Blinking lightly beneath a lead blanket of grey, overbearing cloud leaking depression. People hiding beneath layers of rubber and wool and leather and thick cream to stop the skin from freezing. Four, five, six layers, then socks, outer socks, outside shoes coated in fat, inside shoes in a bag, wet-weather gear, spikes to stop you falling. This is not weather for living in. What brought the human race here when the Mediterranean beckoned? Weighed down by clothing treading carefully soaked by rainfall walking down streets grey with snow turned slush beneath buildings old, frumpy, weighed down with self-importance and class and the promise of endless penance, built from stone grey with age. Walkways subsiding with the weight of self-satisfied Lutheran repression, grey sky crowding in cutting off sight, queues waiting for red plastic-looking hot dogs coated with yellow mustard served in ubiquitous 7-11s, coldness reaching past the fat and the rubber and the leather, cutting off the extremities of the body, the toes, the fingers, the ears. They go blue – then grey – with cold. Everything everything everything closing in, a great grey blanket of depression and panic. The grey has infected the country, the people, the place, I am not will never be part of this grey, this stultification, this suffocation, *that is why my heart is pounding!*

My girlfriend stood by the car, patient, ready to help should help be needed. She couldn't hear the gathering torrent in my head, the torrent inspired by my martyrdom to her need for national identity. She forced a smile; she was shivering with cold as she waited. I grimaced. 'Are you all right?' she asked.

I looked at her. 'All right?' I shouted silently. 'I'm in prison! I crave freedom! FREEEDOOOOM!!'

She continued smiling, unaware of my racial torment. How could she not see with my eyes? How could she be so complicit in her own delusion? I struggled on, my body screaming defiance:

'Freedom from heating, from smoke, formality, provincialism, architecture, language, nationalism. Freedom from how they dim the lights at six, can't they see there's so little light, all we want is light, we haven't been able to see all day long we need all the help we can get. Freedom from overheated trams, buses, shops, houses – humid from melting clothes, airless from closed windows, smoke-filled from cigarettes. Freedom from deoxygenated air, torrid and tar laden. Freedom from breathing in gulps. Freedom from repulsion – people smoking on the streets, in houses, at restaurants, in meetings. Grey smoke filling the air. Cigarette butts stinking upward from the ice, from the pavement, from ashtrays on the dinner table, from ashtrays littered around restaurants, from bars. Freedom from people stinking, me stinking, of stale tobacco, of other people's nicotine addiction. Freedom from the strain of formality, of dressing for dinner, suits, ties, constant *Skålls*, speeches, handshakes, correct placement of cutlery, rituals, a nation of farmers trying to be middle-class. Freedom from the backward-pulling weight of Lutheran architecture, squat buildings in heavy stone frowning down in judgment next to drab delis and petrol stations next to Stalinist blocks of functionality all grey or dull brown. Freedom from the nasality of the language, its constant singsong, its use of clichéd phrases, the formality of its structure, the high pitch of its delivery, the slurred consonants, the fact that I can't understand it, they speak English don't they? Freedom from blatant nationalism, flags littering the city, decorating cakes and Christmas trees and houses and shops and babies' prams. Freedom from the constant questions – aren't Norwegian women beautiful, aren't the fjords beautiful, aren't the mountains beautiful, isn't it beautiful to be in Norway, we are a small country only four million but we are big, we have had Ibsen and Grieg and Åmundsen and Ullman and Munch and countless ski jumpers, we had the best winter Olympics, in Lillehammer, and have you seen the Holmenkollen ski jump? Freedom from the violence of navigation, the way they elbow me aside on the street or in bars or in shops, unable to think of walking round – the migration from rural to urban, a genetic inability to understand the logistics of city streets or enclosed spaces. Freedom from the constant retro of 1970s fashion – sideburns and vinyl jackets and dusty, used colours tired in their time, now without even the pretence of statement. Freedom from weary, used, blocked, strangled grey aspiring middle-class formality, tireless in patting its own blind back, weighed down with history and genetically imbued tradition – I am suffocating, I need light, I need space, I need to see forward, my heart is not coping, I am not coping, I can't see my way out of this trapped, grey, blind, self-satisfied corner of the world –'

My girlfriend was waiting for my answer. I said:

'I'm fine.'

I wasn't. And now I knew why. Type 'Grey + Panic + Depression' into an internet search engine and pages of reference come up. Everybody knows. Grey must be, has to be, the colour of panic. School uniforms are grey, office clerks wear grey suits, grey and grave are the same sound. The Finns have one of the highest suicide rates in the world and their skies are grey most of the year. Corpses go grey. That's how they are described. Skin that is dying goes grey, that's how it is described. Eyes without mercy – the eyes of the torturer, the executioner, the headmaster – grey, that's how they are described. Blind eyes, they too go grey. The walls of hospitals, mental asylums, prisons, they are painted grey. These things instil panic. They are the end. They are inescapable. They are the walls of institutions, they are punishment, pain, loss of vision, loss of freedom, the inescapable loss of sweet, sweet life. Grey is the colossal weight that brings on palpitations of the heart, hyperventilation, nerves sparking warnings into dead-weight hands, ambulance rides in the middle of the night, panic. That's what the doctors meant when they said to relax, they meant stop panicking, but how can I not panic under so much grey? Small wonder the Vikings raped and pillaged across the world, someone had to pay for all that grey.

My girlfriend climbed in the car and opened the passenger side door with relief: I was still standing, I hadn't fallen yet in the slippery slush. 'Get in,' she said, 'I'll take you home.'

January, some time after 3 pm and the sun has long gone. People slip by on the streets dressed in black leaning into the wind, faces lined by frozen air, moisture leaching from their skin. Some crowd into the government-run wine shop, the *Vinmonopolet*, open nine to five, the only place to buy wine or spirits. Prices overinflated to discourage drinking, my alcohol escape a costly one. Dour buildings line Karl Johann's Gate, the main street. I imagine the city burghers of the previous centuries nodding in pious Nordic agreement at the rows of sensible, non-flashy edifices with tourist shops at street level selling kitsch trash, life-size gnomes and goblin villages. Architects have struggled to create buildings that make the grey sky greyer. Ugly corners almost shapeless poke toward the Oslo Fjord, office blocks glorifying in monotones of grey rectangular regularity. My vision pixilates constantly in the attempt to find something to focus on. Our flat is in one of these blocks, an office redefined into a living space, the windows looking out onto formless buildings painted grey no doubt to keep workers' thoughts inside the workplace.

The TV goes on, a music show with a seventies-looking youth shouting excitedly in nasal singsong about some new Norwegian heavy metal band. The country specialises in jazz but that won't fit this boy's voice it goes through me like a blunt saw and raises the heartbeat even

more – 'Can we turn it off?' I ask. I have liberty now, I'm
sick. The nasal voice stops and a grey silence takes its
place. My sickness is not popular – what can I do, it's not
my fault, it's the country's which, effectively, means it
is my girlfriend's, she is Norwegian, she should say sorry
and let me out of here, but I must hold back, calm down,
the heart is panicking. We will go to dinner later, a
business dinner, potential employers, they want me to
write English for them, it may buck me up calm me down;
she has arranged it she is trying to help but I know what
is coming. I can feel an immense weariness as we dress
for the walk past the bleak, grey, frozen buildings, the
doorways flagged by sputtering oil burners, the leafless
trees, the gnomes, the flags, the Aryan blonde blue-eyed
beauties leaning wrinkled into the wind, all the way to the
humble businessman's mansion. The hallway when we get
there one long line of waiting family, the spoilt children in
their Sunday best white shirts, suits, ties, the fat wife with
the bouffant hair and fox-fur collar, the walk down the
line shaking hands, the first aqua vitae and the obligitory
Skåll. I shake the hands, drink the drink, admire the view
across the street to other grey mansions and hear the
questions – do you like it here in Norway? Do you find
Norway beautiful? Do you find Norwegian women beautiful? And the hidden urgent questioning agenda – we are
the world's best aren't we? we are Aryan beautiful aren't
we? we are not forgotten are we? And I feel myself sinking
into the mire of lost, overwritten, past irrelevance, and my
heart beats for what it knows best – space and clearness

and coast and shiny brash newness and the promise of the morning, any morning, a sunrise, a tomorrow, a future not a past, a future, a future, my heart for a future, in the past there was always a future.

We walk back through slush. I keep my mouth closed in a grim smile, hiding the discomfiture, trying not to think of the thudding telltale heart – where's the raven? Not here. It wouldn't survive, I tell myself, but quietly, quietly. My girlfriend senses, I know she senses; if I try a frail attempt at pleasantry she will hear the lie in my voice, the spite and hate and sheer anger and then where will I sleep? *Splosh* go the shoes in time, sinking into discoloured white, then *schlup* in time as they are pulled out. I think: the sound of greyness permeating into leather and sock in a slow, ever-present Munch scream unheard by the patriots of modern, sodden Norway. The thought cheers me up, I want to share it, nearly do but stop, this is the wrong person, where's a cynic when you need them?

She notices. In a guarded but hopeful voice she lets out a light 'What?' high-pitched with fear and anticipation of the answer. 'Nothing,' I reply, hoping it won't go any further – let it be, let it be, at least until we're inside stripping off again before the tropical electronic heat convinces us we have malaria. She sighs, a good sign, a sign of repression; I'm supposed to take up on the sigh, but I won't, not yet.

I am wrong.

She speaks.

'It's not working,' she says.

The heart stops. First time it has done that in a while but the rest doesn't seem to help it. The brain sparks a hundred different responses all fired by one explosion: panic. It chooses non-committal.

'What's not working?'

I'm not going to let her off lightly.

'Being here.'

This could be good. Perhaps she will suggest getting out. Back, maybe, or at least somewhere with light and life and –

'You being here.'

Splosh. Schlup.

'What do you mean?'

'You know what I mean. You hate it here. You hate me here. I'm not getting what I need.'

Splosh. Schlup.

Panic. So much panic. Where will I go? How will I get there? What will I do? Will I be alone for the rest of my life? Why was I so miserable? Have I been that bad? Have I communicated hatred? Do I hate it that much? Do I hate it more than being alone, more than having to move, more than being dropped?

'That's not true. I don't hate it here. And I don't hate you. I'm just taking time to get used to it.'

'Don't.'

Splosh. Schlup.

'I've just been grumpy. Probably drinking too much. I'll stop. After tonight – I could do with a drink after that dinner – but after tonight. And I'll take up skiing. It'll be fun. I love the snow, I don't know why I haven't done it yet.'

I'm convincing myself.

'I said I've not been getting what I need, I, I . . . We have to talk.'

'Look, it's just a glitch, it happens, it's SAD, it's nothing to do with you, I still, you know, love you.'

'We have to talk. It's not working. There's things I need to say.'

'All right then. Go on.'

'Not now. I need to get home and sleep. We'll speak on the weekend.'

'There's no point putting off –'

'Don't.'

She's crying. Oh God I hate it when she cries. When she cries my sympathy goes to her instead of me; I'll agree with anything she says, it's inbuilt. And then when she finishes crying it will all be over, that's inbuilt in her: she cries away the loss, then it's dealt with. So I can't talk now because if she talks and cries it's finished; she'll decide and I'll agree. But if I wait then nothing will be defined, the moment will stretch out and perhaps break into nothing. My God I don't want to leave, it's already past the winter solstice, the days are getting longer from now on, it might become habitable, and what will I do on my own? Look at the sun?

The office block looms overhead, grey but inviting now that living in it is under threat. Up the stairs we go, echoing with dread. I disregard the thumping in my chest, laboured now and weighty with trepidation, straining to push the blood through reluctant veins. I bounce in the door, look behind to her tear-stained face, ask with a smile:

'Cup of tea?'

Her mouth quivers.

'Chamomile.'

'Of course, of course. You go and have a shower, I'll put the tea on. Is it warm enough in here?'

I am sweating.

'It'll be fine. Don't overdo it, please. It won't make a difference.'

She's gone. The shower turns on. I hold back. I can see her refracted image in the stained glass of the door. I always can, but tonight it looks – unreachable, like that first time. Utterly desirable. I won't overdo it, I won't go in, I'll just think. I need to have suggestions ready, achievement potentials, relationship-focused goals, a whole armament of buzz-word personal counsellor strategies to avoid losing My Significant Other. The sun will rise, the sun will rise.

She drinks the tea in silence, thanks me, climbs into bed. I choose discretion, remove myself to the kitchen alcove to clean the cups. She shouts out:

'Hey?'

BaBumBaBumBaBum.

'Yes?'

'You can still sleep in here.'

'Oh.'

I hadn't thought things had gone that far.

'Thanks. Won't be long.'

I put on pyjamas for the first time since coming here. It seems appropriate until I climb in. She's already asleep but when she wakes I'll be in pyjamas, the statement of distance acquiesced to – yet if I remove them now she'll wake.

They soak the sweat up as I listen to her snore. How can she sleep so well? Has this been a long time coming? What does she mean when she says, 'It's not working, you being here'? Not working for me, or for her? God knows, I've tried, I've nearly become alcoholic in the attempt, I've just spent four days in hospital on the edge of death, for heaven's sake. Granted, that doesn't bode well for my ability to live here – but surely it points to my commitment? Now is not the time to end things. If that's where she's going it must've been planned in advance – and planned to make the most possible impact. Kicking a dog when it's down. How dare she? That's so . . . *Norwegian* of her. They're such a pious, insular, excluding, self-righteous race, it'd be typical if she wanted to break up now that she's settled here. It's because I'm not Norwegian. And never will be, thank God! Maybe she's right, in a twisted sort of way, maybe we should break up, I've just never seen her for what she is, the reality of her socio-genetic make-up in context.

I wake to the feel of her palm on my forehead. She sits on the side of the bed in her dressing gown, a tray with breakfast on her lap. She smiles, sadly I think, and hands the tray over. The dressing gown opens slightly. I can see the nipples on her tiny breasts. They seem to have darkened. I look away too late: she pulls the gown tight, sighs.

'I'll make dinner tonight when I get home from work,' she says. 'I'll bring a good bottle of wine back, and we'll talk. Okay?'

'Okay,' I say, and smile. This is all too fast.

'I've had breakfast. I thought I should let you sleep.'

'Okay. Thanks.'

She gets dressed whilst I eat. I sneak the odd look. I can't tell if it's lust, or the desire to capture the final images in case of enforced future celibacy. She affects not to notice.

'I'll be back around six. Look after yourself. Don't stress.'

I snort. She frowns, grimaces, a tear forms, falls.

'Please, you don't understand how hard this is. I'm involved too. I'll see you tonight.'

And she's gone, quickly. I am left in the wrong.

I get up in the afternoon and look at the sheets damp with perspiration. I should change them but it's too much effort, I'll leave them uncovered so they dry. My pyjamas reek of sickness but their clamminess is comforting so I cover the stink with a blanket, wipe the hair from my eyes, and go in search of wine. There is none: she's cleaned the place out. I check through the carton of empty bottles, taking them out to glean the last drops, but they've been washed. Today will be torture.

I wander the few steps to the chair by the window and look out at the office blocks. There are two of them in my vision – one new building with roughly defined concrete lines jutting into space, the other older, more rounded, its facia rotting in the rain. Between them a city street, pavement hidden under ice, road blocked with construction works. The dull roar of machinery can be heard. If they pulled everything down and started again, I think, we might be fine. Or if we could hold out until the summer, the return of light. That's what we should be doing: hibernating. How can anyone survive this climate? And with a Lutheran outlook? Winter in Norway is *designed* to be hell, or at least purgatory; it's not meant for love or passion. She had no right to insist we stay here through winter. 'You'll get to know the real me,' she'd said. I don't *want* to know the real her. I want the fantasy one, the exotic one, the foreign one. Isn't that what we all want? Isn't that why we read, go to the movies, watch TV, go to the theatre, drink, take drugs, travel? Don't we spend most of our lives trying to avoid reality? So why the sudden need to present it? Isn't avoidance the one true benefit of being white middle-class, and isn't that why everyone wants to be white middle-class?

I take a breath, and try to put myself in her shoes. There has to be a reason beyond blind, unreasonable, incomprehensible national pride for her to want to live here. Compared to the Sydney we left – parties, beaches, sunlight, laughter – this is a self-righteous bed of nails, can't she see that? 'Just give it a try,' she'd said. 'It's not as raw over there. There's a cycle. You might like it.' What had she meant? I hadn't thought about it much at the time. I just thought the country might be exotic, like her.

Raw. Now I think about it, I remember when we first arrived, she'd said: 'I feel safe here. I always wondered why women in Sydney didn't wear purdah. I can walk with my head up here.'

So. She'd felt unsafe. But if she'd only said so, we could have moved. We were in the Inner West – what did she expect? The lumpen proletariat kept filtering through, their lizard brains and doctored cars out of control. We could've moved east, that would've solved it. And what did she mean by cycle? Life cycle probably, she always complained about the lack of proper seasons. Difficult to believe that this endless grey is part of what she wants but maybe that's genetic, I have to allow it. But more memories are returning. Conversations at dinner parties, her voice, now I recollect it, tinged with bitterness. I'd always interpreted it as wit. How cutting she would be about the lack of services, the failing transport system, the backward technology, the potholed roads and crumbling buildings fading under the blinding, ozone-free sky. I never thought she *meant* it; it all seemed fine to me. And how dismissive she'd been of what she once called the thin crust of derivative culture – and how loud I'd laughed. Asked once to describe what she thought of the Australian accent, she'd said it reminded her of the yapping of a cornered terrier. I'd thought she was being funny. Had I been deaf? Blind? Had I subconsciously chosen to ignore the signs? There was a night shortly before she suggested moving to Oslo, a night that we 'made love' – an embarrassing cliché, but the act was so tender the words seem to fit. When it was over, she'd said:

'You know, when we first met, in Greece, I thought you were so care-free. In context, I think it's more care-less.'

She'd smiled, I'd laughed. She'd hugged me, gently. At the time, I thought it was a compliment. Now it looks more like a turning point. Context, there's the rub. We are only exotic out of context. I couldn't see her Sydney, she can't see my Oslo. Our separate comfort zones are each other's Orwellian public school. But we had been so good together – we had, I wasn't wrong, those memories were real. Surely they were. Do we have to let go of that tiny, exhilarating, energising world-of-two, each fading back into our own mutually exclusive context? Won't that be a major defeat, the ultimate conservative choice? Is there no other way out?

And then it hits me. It is so obvious. We have the capability, for a year at least, the money's low but I can make it stretch. We will travel. The one ruling principle –

never touch a country either can communicate in. We will experience the exotic – go to South America, to Africa, to Eastern Europe. We will live cheaply, find the fantasy in each other, that unknown that drew us together in the first place. No more dark grey Lutheran Norway, no more blinding bright redneck Australia; just newness, constant fresh newness. That is my plan, my buzz-word strategy for relationship renewal. My heart reacts: it settles, back to its living beat, it has found the crack between the walls to bring it outside and there is no hell, the sun will rise. I rush to the computer and go to Google heaven: cheap flights to Rio De Janeiro as a start. I create an itinerary, driving fearlessly through the military dicta-torships of the Third World: bound to make us feel superior, better, richer, more interesting, and mutually desirable. It is a win-win situation, there's no way she can refuse. Who would want to stay here in the frozen waste-lands of the Protestant north when the sunlit fantasy is so easy to reach?

I stop and look up as I hear the door open. I see her instant reaction: the nose wrinkle at the sweat; the eyes flick over the damp unmade bed, the scattered empty bottles, my pyjamas and dressing gown. She opens her mouth to speak, but I beat her to it.

'It doesn't matter!' I shout, 'I have a plan! Wait until you hear!'

She puts down her bags and I can't help but hear the welcome *clink* of bottles in the blue *Vinmonopolet* bags. What an exciting, cozy, rejuvenating evening awaits us.

'I'm pregnant,' she says.

That's a shock. I look at her, surprised, but my brain works hard and fast. The last few hours have been revelatory. I've begun to understand how much I love this woman, how much I enjoy being with her, so long as it's not here. And I feel for her now, I forgive her: I had been so uncaring back in Sydney, so wilfully unaware of the signals she was sending my way. I need to let her know, to make up for my lack of listening, to tell her we have the ability to rediscover what we had. True, pregnancy hadn't crossed my mind. We have never discussed children, at least not in detail – she might have mentioned a desire to have one, but it's never gone further than that. I don't know if this is the best timing, or what her attitude to abortion is, but either way it doesn't affect anything. We can deal with it in many ways – and if she wants to keep it – well – we can still travel – for six months at least – and maybe a child will be another form of fantasy – the world through growing eyes – we can be 'world-of-three' – our shared DNA uniting us – strengthening the cross-hemisphere link that first pulled us together on the party islands of Greece – it could be so good. It can work! It can!

Then it hits me: we haven't had sex for a while. I pause.

'How?' I ask.

Love and Death in Darlinghurst

MANDY SAYER

When we began to fall in love, he was still living with his wife. The process was so gradual it was almost imperceptible, like watching trees flower. I didn't have much time to contemplate what was unfolding between us because my thoughts were elsewhere: my father was sleeping in my bed every night, while I lay on the floor in the next room, listening to his faltering breath, the short sharp wheezing after he spat blood into a bucket.

Louis and I met several weeks before my father's diagnosis. A friend, Linda Jaivin, threw a dinner party and the other two invited guests pulled out at the last moment. A phone call later, Louis arrived to fill out the numbers, all long limbs and wild black curly hair as he bounded through the door. He didn't seem so much a man as a force of nature, a whirlwind of stories, one-liners and witticisms that were seemingly inexhaustible. Over pita bread and red wine we chatted about the area in which we both lived – Kings Cross – and how so many of Australia's most prominent writers had either lived in the Cross and/or written about it. By the time Linda served the entree, the three of us had decided to edit an anthology about the Cross. Of course, like most writers, I'd participated in many a boozy, potentially great collaborative idea before, and assumed that the excitement of this prospective project would soon fade the following day, along with our hangovers.

The next morning Louis faxed me to arrange a meeting. By the time the three of us convened at Moran's café to sketch out a structure for the book, Linda confessed she had to drop out of the project, due to pressing deadlines. I felt conflicted myself. Apart from working on a screenplay, a short story collection and trying to finish my doctorate, my father had just been diagnosed with lung cancer and given six months to live. I would be his only carer.

I had turned up to the meeting prepared to bow out of the project too.

But Linda made her announcement first, and when I expressed doubts about my own availability, Louis flashed me a look of such profound disappointment that I qualified my excuses and simply warned him that, during the editing process, my energies would be stretched.

We drew up a reading list and parted ways. My time over the following months was divided between measuring morphine, counting tablets, reading works by Kenneth Slessor and Sumner Locke Elliot, revising my story collection, daily walks with my father to St Vincent's Hospital for his radiotherapy treatment, organising blood transfusions, researching the history of Kings Cross, and struggling, with great difficulty, to keep my nerve. Louis and I would meet about once a week, at Moran's, to exchange material, and to discuss and shape what was becoming our manuscript. I soon found, however, that he was a speed reader and I could not keep up with the pace at which he devoured entire books. I, on the other hand, am slow and careful, rereading paragraphs, making notes in the margin. I felt guilty about not being able to keep up with him.

At one point, after I'd taken my father to the Emergency department of St Vincent's, and been informed that the cancer had spread to his lymph nodes, I faxed Louis and explained, with great regret, that I could no longer cope and had to pull out of the project altogether. Perhaps he could find a replacement, or continue with the editing on his own?

He called me immediately: he understood the pressure I was under, but wanted me to remain attached to the anthology. He would do most of the initial reading, and I would eventually vet his short list. *Just turn up to Moran's, have a glass of wine, and give me your opinions*, he said with his usual jollity. This seemed simple enough, but I still felt uneasy about not being able to make an equal contribution.

Sometimes I'd turn up tense as a stretched piano string, faltering and out of tune with the project. The cancer had travelled up to my father's frontal lobe, which stimulated aggressive behaviour, and his usual warm and genial manner had calcified into persistent vitriol: his food was never hot enough, his enemas weren't effective, all his doctors were idiots, and there was no way he was going to let a visiting palliative care nurse through the door to check his blood count and weight. It was the first time he'd ever yelled at me, and he continued to yell at me often. My greatest fear was that he would die, disappointed in and withholding his love from me.

Louis and I talked as much about these problems as we did the virtues of Kenneth Mackenzie's novel *The Refuge*, and the deficits of Patrick White's strained, lumpy prose. Anecdotes of incontinence dovetailed into a shared passion for Jon Rose's 1940s novel *At the Cross*, and these meetings slowly acquired the ambience of respite, throwing a small beam of light into my grief and diminishing stamina. The wine was a kind of medicine, and Louis made me laugh so much the knot in my stomach loosened into a tranqil warmth. I guess it was inevitable that, over time, he would share some of his own problems with me.

One afternoon, after polishing off a bottle of white, Louis confessed that his marriage was in trouble. He had married just over two years before in the hope that it would renew the relationship, but he found he and his wife were growing even more apart. Of course, I found this puzzling, but when I questioned him further about it, he was evasive and changed the subject. I concluded that each relationship has its particular problems and secrets, and decided not to press him for further details or an explanation.

My father's condition worsened: he grew thin and gaunt, refused to bathe, and barked at me relentlessly. He complained of a gnawing pain in his stomach and, after I took him to the Emergency ward again for treatment, he was admitted to St Vincent's Hospice. It was during this period that I asked Louis if he would shoot some video footage of my father. Gerry was fading away, from the world, from his own life, and from me. I loved him deeply and needed to create a keepsake.

Gerry was wary of Louis at first, as he was of any man who might compete for his daughter's attention. But as the filming progressed, Louis slowly won him over with his humour and lack of guile. Gerry was impressed by Louis' snappy suits and snakeskin boots, and by his habit of always turning up to these sessions with a bottle of Seagrams gin. By the third afternoon of shooting, we three were like a trio of old raconteurs, sipping martinis on the balcony of the hospice and trading stories with one another.

I'd put Gerry to bed at eight o'clock, kiss him goodnight and turn out the light. That was always the hardest time of my day, leaving him behind and closing the door, not knowing if he'd still be alive when I returned in the morning. Louis would walk me home, his slender arm wrapped around me, as if I were too young or confused to cross a busy city street on my own.

Gerry survived the first stroke. When he regained consciousness after a twelve-hour coma, I realised his personality had changed yet again, and the sweet and genial man I had known all my life returned. He was calm and affectionate. He began smoking cigars and his sense of humour ran riot. When the hospital barber entered his shared ward and asked if anyone needed a haircut, Gerry retorted, in his loudest voice, *I'll have a shampoo and a blow job*! When he saw a fellow patient kissing the resident cat on the mouth – a patient whom he loathed – he declared with great glee, *Do you know that just five minutes ago that cat was licking its arse*?

The doctor explained to me that the stroke had provided a minor lobotomy on his frontal lobe, essentially zapping out his aggressive behaviour. Some afternoons he'd leave the hospice wearing my purple satin pyjamas, and walk down the street to the Darlo Bar, where he'd sink a few schooners and hold court with the local bar flies. He was released from the hospice between Christmas and New Year, 1999, painfully thin, yet optimistic. He had so little weight on him that, as I was unlocking the door to my building, a blast of wind blew him over.

During this time, Louis and I met more frequently, over lunch, sometimes dinner. The pretext was our anthology project, but it was hard not to notice that something had changed between us, even though, at the time, neither of us could have named it. In spite of the fact that he was dying, my father noticed this too, and he surprised me by broaching the subject early one afternoon. *Why don't you two get together? You're bloody made for one another.*

I nodded briefly and sighed. *There's only one problem,* I replied – *he's married.*

This, however, did not deter my father, who had never lived by any sense of morality but his own.

The last of our film sessions was in my apartment, early on New Year's Eve – a fresh bottle of gin, jazz on the stereo – only hours before the dawn of the new millennium. Whenever I left the room I could overhear my father prodding Louis: *Why haven't you made a pass at my daughter? Isn't she beautiful? You two are made for one another.* Each time he did this I flushed with embarrassment, but I couldn't help admiring him for his dogged effort to nudge us together.

Before Louis left that night, he walked into the bathroom, where I was washing my hands, took me in his arms and kissed me deeply, and I kissed him back, inhaling his delicious, lime-tinged scent.

Ten days later, as I was handing my father his morning medication, his body stiffened, his eyes rolled back and he fell into my arms, trembling violently, as if he were having an epileptic fit.

I rode with him in the ambulance and, after he was

admitted to Emergency, I was taken to a small room where a doctor told me that he'd had a second, more serious stroke and could die at any time. I had him transferred to the hospice, where I knew he would receive the medication and care that would allow him to pass away as painlessly as possible.

I was supposed to have a meeting with Louis that afternoon and rang him to cancel. Within fifteen minutes, he was sitting by me at Gerry's bedside, pouring me a glass of wine and holding my hand. It was the most comfort and support I'd received from anyone I knew – including my relatives.

When Gerry regained consciousness, it was obvious even to him that he had very little time left. He'd lost his motor coordination and was now unable to feed himself or go to the bathroom, though he was able to hold a glass of wine in his trembling hands, to raise it to his mouth.

For a long time he held my free hand, repeatedly lifting it to his lips and kissing my fingers, my knuckles, over and over, like some dashing, medieval knight.

Yes, Gerry, I said, *there's not enough kissing in the world.*

No, he replied, glancing directly at Louis, and then at me, *there's not enough fucking in the world.*

It was the last lucid comment he would ever make.

Now, my father would always be unavailable to me, and our relationship would forever be circumscribed by the greatest distance of them all. Louis had videotaped part of Gerry's final hours, how he'd wheezed into an oxygen mask, the way he'd held my hand and gazed at me sorrowfully with glazed blue eyes. Hours later, after he fell into a coma, a nurse wheeled in a fold-out bed for me so I could sleep beside him through the night. And Louis lay down with me for a long time, gathering me in his arms, stroking my hair. We kissed once or twice and then I passed out, exhausted by the twelve-hour vigil.

Louis was the last person to see my father alive. When he rose at midnight, Gerry seemed to be breathing and sleeping peacefully. An hour after Louis went home, however, my father finally and quietly slipped away, while I slept on, oblivious of his passing.

His funeral took place six days later, on a glorious sunny day in the middle of summer. In the meantime, I had to make the arrangements, inform family and friends, publish notices, and did not have the time or energy to meet with Louis and discuss what was unfolding between us. Even though my father had obviously given Louis and me an unconditional blessing, I felt conflicted about falling for an unavailable man and, of course, I was grieving and needed time alone.

The service was wild and joyful, as had been my father's life. I organised a five-piece jazz band to play in the church, which was packed with musicians, actors, bar flies and relatives. After we carried the coffin out to the car, the band and congregation filed onto the footpath and followed the hearse down Darlinghurst Road, which the police had closed off, all playing percussion instruments along with the saxophonist's fast blues. The hearse turned

left into Liverpool Street and the living repaired to the
Darlo Bar for the wake. All this Louis filmed for me; these
tapes would become a tender and moving memento of the
last days of one important relationship for me and,
though I hardly knew it then, the early ones of yet another.

He shadowed me during the wake like a chaperone,
alert to any possible needs, buying me drinks, making
sure I didn't lose my handbag. He was infinitely more
supportive than anyone in my family and I found myself
drawn to him like a plant straining for sunlight.

My mother was playing the bereaved widow, even
though she and my father had been legally separated for
over twenty-seven years and she now had an adult son
fathered by another man. She howled against the chests
of my father's old friends, some of whom she'd had flings
with decades earlier.

When a fight between my brothers threatened to
derail the evening, I invited friends back to my apartment
and asked Louis if he could walk my tipsy mother home.
He later told me she'd flirted with him in the lift and, as
he guided her towards my front door, she turned and
leaned against him. *Don't get involved with Mandy*,
she warned. *She's very promiscuous.* Inside, my sister
collapsed in his arms, crying, while my irate younger
brother was ready to thump Louis a couple of times for
taking advantage of his sister.

After a few hours of this kind of hysteria, I murmured
to Louis, *Let's get out of here*. We walked arm-in-arm
through the main streets of Kings Cross, through pleats

of neon and pulsing lights, past hookers teetering on platform shoes, strip club spruikers, weaving drunks, a teenage girl trying to sell a tarnished charm bracelet. As we strolled I realized I felt completely alienated from my family and their behaviour. Not one of them had helped me care for Gerry during his illness, yet now they were squabbling over his few possessions: his kit of drums, his CDs, his few pieces of jewellery. What perplexed me the most was that, during his last weeks, Gerry had worked so hard to ensure I would inherit some kind of happiness after his passing, yet it seemed my relatives were now trying to undermine his efforts. It propelled me away from them and even closer to Louis, who, with his arm tight around my waist, felt more familiar to me than any one of my siblings or my mother. It wasn't that he felt like home; it was more intense than that: to me, the man already *was* home. Unfortunately, he had a home of his own, and it certainly wasn't where I lived.

That night he walked me back to my apartment and lay beside me in bed, his long arms around me as I pressed into his curly black chest hair. When I woke the next morning I was surprised to see him still there beside me, gazing out the window at the harbour's sequins of light. As I wiped the crust out of my eyes, he announced, very quietly, that he intended to separate from his wife. This of course was a surprise, given that we'd never had sex and, as far as I was concerned, weren't about to any time soon, but an even bigger surprise was imminent: he was going to discuss it with her today, that very morning, if possible.

I replied that the choice was his, but begged him to postpone the discussion. Gerry's death, the funeral, and the fallout with my family was more stress than I could manage in the space of a single week.

Louis merely replied, half-smiling, *I agree with your father – there's not enough fucking in the world.*

That afternoon he moved out of his apartment and into his Edgecliff office, where he would live for the next four weeks.

In early February, we took our first brief holiday together, at the sprawling Carrington Hotel in the Blue Mountains. After we checked in, we were handed the keys to a room furnished with antiques. It opened onto a balcony affording breathtaking views of swirling mist and deep, moss-green valleys. Since the school holidays were now over, the hotel was virtually empty and, that morning, as we explored the winding staircases, the wide halls, the games room and library, we encountered no one. It was as if all the privacy and time we had yearned for over the months had been offered to us all at once, as if we were the owners of this vast, sumptuous palace, and the bar waiter, the desk clerk, the chef, were merely part of our personal entourage. It was also a relief to be away from Sydney, and the speculative eyes of people not accustomed to seeing Louis and me arm-in-arm.

We were sweeping through the bar late on our first

afternoon when we finally ran into two other guests: I did a double-take and realised that not only did I know this couple, the man, nicknamed Smedley, was an old family friend and had played the bass at my father's funeral, only two weeks earlier. He and his wife, Tess, were staying at the hotel, celebrating their tenth wedding anniversary. They insisted that we join them for dinner that night in the Carrington's dining room, to help them celebrate. So much for anonymity.

Upstairs, Louis and I made love for the first time. Afterwards, he lay beside me in bed and read aloud from one of his favourite novels, Carson McCullers' *The Member of the Wedding*. It felt delicious to be snuggled in bed, listening to the cadences of his voice, the smell of his sweat on my skin. It was the first time in many months that I'd felt something close to joy.

Afterwards, we dressed and joined Tess and Smed in the grand dining room. The four of us were the only guests seated for dinner. A concert piano gleamed in one corner; chandeliers twinkled above; the hundred or so other tables sat mute beneath cloaks of white linen, all of which reinforced this sense that Louis and I were Lord and Lady of the Manor. Within minutes, however, another couple – both of whom were in their late sixties – were seated in the middle of the room. We soon found out they, too, were celebrating a wedding anniversary – their fortieth – and had travelled from Canada to commemorate it at the same hotel in which they'd spent their honeymoon.

By the end of the second course, I'd invited them over to join us for a drink. A shy, grinning teenager, on his first day as a waiter, kept dropping plates and tubs of butter, and continued to return to our table with bottles of champagne for which he kept forgetting to bill us. A local woman appeared, as if from nowhere and, unannounced, sat at the piano and began playing Beethoven's Fifth Symphony with impeccable timing and tone. The Canadian man boasted that he'd sung to his new bride in this very room on their honeymoon, in February 1960, which was three years before I was born.

What was the song? I asked.

'*Some Enchanted Evening*'.

I whispered in the pianist's ear and soon had the Canadian up on his feet, crooning a rendition to his teary wife.

It felt oddly coincidental and yet somehow prophetic that this was my first real 'date' with Louis. Afterwards, I overheard Smedley remarking to the pianist, *Those two are celebrating their fortieth, me and Tess our tenth, and these two*, he added, waving his hand at me and Louis, *these two are just starting out.*

I was renting an apartment in Kings Cross that was so small my writing desk was wedged into a corner of the only bedroom. It didn't occur to either of us that Louis could possibly move in with me. When the lease expired on his office he rented an apartment which was only a two-minute walk away from my flat, around the corner in Kellett Street. He had no furniture or utensils – having left everything with his wife, and so I filled his kitchen with some of Gerry's old pots and crockery, his iron, his bar fridge, a mirror. It was strange to open the cupboards and see the shot glasses, the floral plates, the Irish coffee mugs that had been part of my father's home for over a decade, here in this strange, new environment. I also gave him one of my couches and a large oriental coffee table. The only thing he had to buy was a fold-out sofa bed, pillows and an eiderdown.

I felt bad that he'd given up so much in order to end his marriage: a two-bedroom apartment with panoramic harbour views way out to the Heads, his videos and CDs, his paintings and photographs, even his adored chihuahua, Ren. (A few months after Louis separated from his wife, Ren was hit by a car and killed.) Now Louis was living in a small, rented apartment on a block populated with brothels and a legalised heroin injecting room. But he didn't seem to mind at all; in fact he seemed elated: *I don't care where I live*, he said, *as long as I can write.*

The short distance between his home and mine worked well for us both in the beginning. Louis began cooking at night, either at my place or his, and we settled into a quiet, domestic routine. Having had a history of insomnia, however, I soon found I couldn't sleep well unless I was at home, and so we began spending most nights at my apartment in my high, queen-sized bed.

Now that we could enjoy more time together, we began to introduce each other to our respective interests and hobbies. Louis, a natural athlete, tried to teach me how to play tennis, but even when I wore my glasses I could rarely hit the ball. He grew tired of waiting as I chased after it, or when I batted the racket against nothing but air as I continued to miss my own serve. After three attempted 'lessons' he never raised the subject of tennis again. Similarly, I was interested in learning swing and jive dancing and signed us both up for a ten-week course. Five minutes into the first lesson, however, I realised I'd made a fatal mistake: Louis didn't know his left foot from his right, kept coming in on the wrong beat, and when he'd spin me around he'd invariably trip me up. I was relieved to leave the hall that night and, like the tennis lessons, we both silently agreed to drop the idea.

A great fan of football and cricket, Louis was appalled to discover that I had never attended a live sporting event, and was further astonished that I didn't even know the difference between Rugby League and AFL. When he took me to a cricket test match between England and Australia, I made the cardinal sin of mistaking Brett Lee for Shane Warne. It was that day we realised how fortunate we were to be living separately: it soon became obvious to us both that I am a slob and Louis is anally retentive; Louis likes loud hip hop, I prefer jazz; Louis has filled his apartment with chihuahua statues, mine is brimming with scores of vintage shoes.

We continued working on our anthology, organising the material we'd selected into chapters representing every decade of the twentieth century. Sometimes, however, our

professional and personal lives overlapped. One afternoon, I had the selection laid out in rows on the polished
wooden floor of my living room and we were glancing
over the pieces, rearranging the sequence and discussing
cuts for the final draft. Louis was making a comment
about the dearth of Kings Cross literature set in the 1980s,
when I found myself no longer listening to what he was
saying. I pushed him down on the floor, on top of the rows
of manuscript papers, wrapped my limbs around him, and
put my mouth on his. His head was lying against an
excerpt from George Johnston's *Clean Straw for Nothing*;
my arm suddenly elbowed an extract of *Aunts Up the
Cross*, by Robin Dalton. Soon we were rolling over
Patrick White, Betty Roland and Kenneth Slessor, the
sheets beneath us crumpling like a bed of leaves.

This irreverence brimmed over into our first overseas
holiday. Any restraint we'd exercised earlier in our friendship was now completely vanquished. Six months after
the Carrington weekend, Louis took me to Ubud, a town
in the Balinese hills, where we rented a suite in a traditional resort for a week. As the days passed, the staff
grew more and more perplexed because we so rarely left
our room. At lunchtime, we'd order *nasi goreng* and cold
beer through room service. When the meals arrived the
waiter would suggest, politely at first, that he could
organise half- or full-day tours for us: whitewater rafting,
the monkey forest; wouldn't we like to see the silver
mines? With each delivery, we'd graciously yet firmly
decline, until one day an exasperated waiter finally voiced

the collective concern of the resort workers: *Why you no tour? Why you stay in room all day?*

Louis smiled and signed the meal docket. *We're on our honeymoon*, he explained, handing him the pen. The waiter glanced at me and then at Louis. We were both barefoot and wearing white cotton robes. An expression of relief, almost joy, overcame him. He smiled, nodded and backed out of the room. No one at the resort ever bothered us again.

We whiled away the rainy afternoons on our private veranda, overlooking a pond filled with goldfish and watersnakes. The marble bath was so big we could lie side by side in it. I was rereading Marquez's *Love in the Time of Cholera*; Louis was devouring *Julius Caesar*. At night we'd roll around on the bed, amusing each other by making up limericks: I remember during one inspired moment I managed to rhyme *Charles Mingus* with *cunnilingus*.

One day we were wrestling on the floor and Louis picked me up and threw me onto the four-poster bed, the drapes and posts of which suddenly collapsed on top of me, along with Louis, amid peals of raucous laughter. It did feel like a honeymoon and, when we returned to Sydney and our separate homes, I felt a sense of loss. As I unpacked my clothes and sorted my shoes, I was surprised by how much I missed him.

After a year of shuffling back and forth between our two apartments, the unit directly above mine became vacant, and it seemed inevitable that Louis would move into it. The flat had glorious views over Woolloomooloo and the Harbour Bridge and, as we shifted in his furniture, we fantasised about buying both flats and installing a spiral staircase between them. Louis bought a four-poster, queen-sized bed and we would lie in during the mornings, gazing out the window at the peaked sails of the Opera House.

Now, Louis could cook in his kitchen upstairs, bring the meals down on a tray, and serve them on my candle-lit veranda. If I became restless at night trying to sleep in his bed, I could always slip down to mine without disturbing him, much to the delight of one of my neighbours.

Boris lived across the landing from my apartment. He was an overweight, unemployed, English accountant who bore an alarming resemblance to Benny Hill. He occasionally brought home local hookers and had a serious gambling problem. He often left his front door open to *circulate fresh air*. He once confessed to me that he was thrilled to have me and Louis as neighbours. When I asked him why, his eyebrows did a brief, lascivious dance. *I love watching you both running up and down the stairs, half naked!*

Our anthology, *In the Gutter . . . Looking at the Stars*, was published in July 2000 and it was a surprise and a relief that, in spite of death and divorce, the project that had united us initially had finally come to fruition. We toured Sydney, Melbourne and Canberra, promoting and reading from the book.

Of course, like most couples who choose not to cohabit, it was only when we were travelling – and hence briefly living together – that we learned the extent of each other's idiosyncrasies. I soon realised that, as a result of his traumatic childhood, my boyfriend had a pathological dislike of Melbourne, so much so that, when we first spent two days there, the only words he uttered to me or anyone else in those forty-eight hours were during radio and television interviews. On a subsequent trip he refused to eat and became withdrawn and suicidal. A holiday in Byron Bay brought on a panic attack after we bicycled through the rain, and I learned, very quickly, that Louis could not bear to get his hair wet.

Similarly, when we holidayed in Samoa and were assigned a hut right next to a bottling plant, Louis first experienced my neurotic intolerance of white noise. Even the humming of a refrigerator can send me into a rage, so when we woke on our first morning to what sounded like a semitrailer idling outside our door, Louis realised immediately that neither of us would have any peace – let alone sex – until we were relocated to another room. The staff's command of English was mild at best, only slightly better than their organisational skills. After two days of begging to be transferred, Louis finally told the front desk clerk that he was writing a travel article on Samoa and the hotel for the *Sydney Morning Herald*.

Suddenly, we were moved from the worst hut on the island to the best suite in the resort, a huge apartment with a wide patio overlooking the Pacific Ocean. By that time, however, I was seriously ill, with vomiting, fever and dizziness.

Louis remained in the living room most of the time, reading up on Samoan history, while I lay in bed watching reruns of the only movie that we could access on the hotel's network, *Pay it Forward*, a story about generating good deeds. Soon I discovered that, because of all the mosquitoes in our first hut, I had contracted dengue fever. Our great romantic week descended into days of sweat-stained sheets and frequent rushes to the bathroom. I put away our various sex toys in the bedside drawer, where they remained for the rest of our stay. I felt guilty about this but Louis didn't seem to mind.

I could no longer hold down any food, so he patiently ordered up martinis and Panadol and brought them to my side. He was amused by the fact that several American FBI agents would be moving into our suite when we checked out at the end of the week. The agents were coming to investigate a series of local murders, and Louis managed to make several jokes about it. His serene and uncomplaining nature, under such dire circumstances, made me love and admire him even more.

His serenity, however, was further tested when we were flying back to Sydney. About two hours into our flight, his joints began to ache and he broke into a sweat. He complained of nausea and a headache; as he was elaborating on his symptoms, I suddenly sat bolt upright and cried, *Oh shit!*

What's up? he asked.

I assumed he'd be angry with me, and was ambivalent about telling him what was on my mind.

Are you okay? he persisted. *What's wrong?*

I swallowed and shifted in my seat. *The sex toys,* I said. *I left them in the bedside drawer.*

Louis frowned, then pursed his lips. I was waiting for him to berate me for being so forgetful, but he merely shook his head briefly and burst into laughter. *Well, the FBI's going to have a good time tonight!*

Louis' divorce papers were signed in December 2001, and he was left with less than a third of his former assets. Still, he seemed more optimistic and contented than ever, as if money and property were self-renewing entities that required little or no attention. Again, his grace and confidence impressed me: he went about his work each day with the same amount of intense concentration and happiness. I always knew when he was writing well because there'd be no footsteps above my head, no music, no whistling kettle – just the silence of someone ensconced in an imaginary world, the quietude of a man dreaming.

He proposed to me on my birthday: St Valentine's Day, 2002. Instead of popping the question with an engagement ring, he instead proffered a one-off black

Armani dress and matching high-heeled Italian shoes, both of which fitted perfectly. I could hardly have declined after such a thoughtful and romantic gesture. The distance between us was gradually narrowing, both literally and figuratively, and the closeness we now enjoyed was almost visceral in its intensity.

One afternoon, Boris stopped me on the stairs and told me he had to sell his apartment immediately so he could move back to England and into the home of his ageing parents. I inspected the unit on my own initially, and found posters of topless biker chicks on the walls and, in the study, a list of Boris's most recent resolutions thumbtacked to a pin board: *lose 15 kilos, blood pressure down by a third; no more betting (except for the Spring Carnival and the Davis Cup); pay off Visa interest; no more women (except Irene on the weekends and Debbie when she comes up from Wollongong)*. It wasn't hard to intuit that Boris was in desperate financial straits and, that afternoon, Louis and I offered a ludicrously cheap price for the apartment, which a relieved Boris hastily accepted. The night before Boris was due to fly out of Sydney, he invited us to his farewell dinner in a local pub. Seated beside him was an attractive blonde 'masseuse', who was accompanying him on a week-long holiday to the Cook Islands before he flew on alone to London. To help finance this jaunt, he explained, we had to pay for our own plates of spaghetti.

Within a month Louis was living directly across the landing from me, only four footsteps away. Now he didn't have to negotiate the stairs when serving dinner, or tiptoe around on his hardwood floors. He set about installing floor-to-ceiling bookshelves throughout the apartment to contain his voluminous library. Whenever we threw a party the celebrations would start in his apartment and spill over into mine. Late one night he was in a mischievous mood and dared me to walk naked from one apartment to the other. His only disappointment was that no one else in the building saw me skipping across the landing.

Eventually, I collected my father's ashes from the Eastern Suburbs Memorial Park. Gerry had specified that he wanted to be cremated but had not told me what he wanted done with his remains. I thought about scattering them at Coogee Beach, where I'd swum with him as a child, or beneath his favourite tree in the Royal Botanic Gardens. Until I could make up my mind, I decided to store the ashes in an oriental urn. At the crematorium, I passed the urn over to the clerk; she nodded and disappeared into another room. When she returned about ten minutes later, she had the urn in one hand and a rectangular cardboard box in the other. *Dad didn't quite fit into the urn*, she explained, *he was too big*! When I arrived home, I placed the urn on top of the box in an antique cabinet with bevelled glass panels, along with the last bottle of gin we three had shared only days before Gerry died. There were still several shots left in it.

Louis and I were married in St John's Anglican Church in Darlinghurst on 2 February 2003, three years after my father's passing. The church was only one block away from where he'd died. Most of the relatives and friends who'd been sceptical of our union initially were there at the service, and my mother even refrained from making a second pass at my groom. The band that had performed at my father's funeral played during the service. Instead of the wedding march, the pianist played the old jazz standard, 'Our Love Is Here to Stay' on the century-old pipe organ while an old family friend walked me down the aisle. Instead of hymns, singer Jeff Duff led the congregation in a rendition of Stevie Wonder's 'You Are the Sunshine of My Life' and Gershwin's ''S Wonderful'. I was amused to glance back and see everyone in my family belting out the lyrics on the left-hand side of the church, while Louis' relatives, sequestered on the right, stood in silent and embarrassed bemusement. After the vows were exchanged, the Reverend recited the Lord's Prayer and fluffed one of the lines: *Lead us into temptation . . .*

After the service, we *were* led into temptation, with Jeff Duff and the musicians as our leaders: Louis, I and the guests followed them, pied piper-like, out of the church and through the streets of Kings Cross, past the looming red-and-white Coca Cola sign at the top of William Street, the seedy Fishbowl Bar, the elderly prostitute with the cat's-eye glasses, saxophones wailing, tambourines jingling, drums booming, even managing to pick up one or two street people along the way. We rounded corners, stopped traffic, and eventually marched into the Bayswater Brasserie for champagne, seafood and speeches.

My favourite moment of the celebrations was towards the end of the night, when I glanced up to see our tipsy Reverend on the dance floor, his crucifix swinging wildly from a chain around his neck as the band played Nine Inch Nails' 'I Want to Fuck You Like An Animal'. A fitting transition from the wedding to the honeymoon.

We spent a week on the coast of Western Australia, just a few miles from the wine-making district of Margaret River. I swam in the wild surf, Louis read, and some days we'd hire a taxi for the day to take us touring through the various wineries. Still, I managed to exasperate Louis that week by accidentally smashing several glasses and breaking the suite's wide-screen television set. *Thank God we don't live together*, he murmured, *I wouldn't have anything left*! He threatened to buy me a set of plastic glasses and plates, and to keep me on a leash if I've consumed more than three glasses of wine.

We divided our wedding gifts and returned to our respective apartments.

Louis, the official cook, took all the kitchenware. Due to a drastic shortage I, the official klutz, claimed the several sets of glasses.

Now that we were married, we briefly contemplated the idea of sharing the one home – a house, possibly, with a garden shed for a writing studio. But after a long, objective look at Louis' apartment – stuffed with chihuahua tea towels, mugs, statues, and calendars; shelves of books on the porn star Christie Canyon, another set of shelves devoted to tomes on the history of mushrooms; his CD collection filled with the names of bands I could hardly pronounce – I wasn't sure it was a good idea. He, too, felt the same when he considered my swing music, the pink walls of my living room, my many hats and shoes, my fridge almost crawling with moulding containers of food.

A year after we married, we purchased a larger apartment just around the corner from our building, a two-bedroom home where I could enjoy my own study and have enough room for a dining table and piano. Louis now cooks dinner in my kitchen and mostly sleeps in my bed at night. He rises early and leaves before I wake at around 10 am, and we each enjoy a full day of silence to write uninterrupted. We often email funny, loving, or even lustful messages to each other throughout our day, and it's exciting to meet up in the evenings and go out on a date.

After I moved into the new apartment, I bought a snare drum, similar to the one my father played. I opened the oriental urn and the cardboard box and tipped the grey and grainy ashes into the drum, filled the airhole with Spakfilla, then sealed up the skin. Whenever we have a dinner party now, we always end up around the piano singing old jazz tunes, while I or another guest plays the snare, and sometimes, as my husband refills my glass, he likes to imitate the nasally voice of his dead father-in-law: *There's not enough fucking in the world.*

The Italian Job

TOM GLEESON

Ellie Parker loves her name. I love Ellie Parker's name. Ellie is short for nothing. She has no middle name and with the surname Parker, she sounds like the love interest of a superhero. At the time of writing there is a film coming out soon called *Ellie Parker*, starring Naomi Watts. I told Ellie that it is just a matter of time before she does not have her name to herself any more. She might as well be called Erin Brockovich or Bridget Jones. When she tells people her name, 'What a lovely name' is going to switch to 'You mean like the movie?' I try to give Ellie hope by saying that maybe the film will flop and disappear without a trace but she assures me that it won awards at the Sundance Film Festival so she is doomed. I am quite selfishly upset because people might think that this story is about my long distance love with a movie and not my Ellie Parker.

I am a stand-up comic. I spend months at a time on tour, sometimes travelling the world. This is a whole lot of fun for me. I get to do what I love and see the world at the same time. Life does not get much more simple than turning up to a town, making them laugh and then moving on. This is not a whole lot of fun for Ellie Parker. She is infinitely more intelligent and sophisticated than me. I always feel guilty when I am overseas because I know that she would get more out of the experience than I do. Yet she waits at home in her regular life for me to get back. At the law firm where she works, her day is punctuated by phone calls from me telling her how much fun I am having on tour and how I do not miss being home at all.

I met Ellie Parker at university. It was at a friend's cast party. We were both hangers-on. We found ourselves quite happy to chat to each other for hours, not letting anyone else in for a bite at the conversation. The chat was chock-full of philosophy, sarcasm, my passion for comedy and her two passions, food and speaking Italian. I was showing off to this impressionable eighteen-year-old with all of my twenty-one-year-old wisdom. I wanted to meet up again but she was playing it cool. I wrote in her diary to meet under the jacaranda in the main quadrangle at lunch on Tuesday. After that we used to run into each other every day for lunch but we never made a time or place. For some reason, formalising the structure would ruin it. Yet every lunchtime would play out the same way. We would run into each other at our favourite café, eat lunch on a lawn then miss afternoon lectures because we were chatting too much. We were making amazing discoveries. 'I can't believe that we agree about music, films, politics and religion! Are we going to have an argument ever?' Then Ellie would agree that yes I was quite interesting. As far as she was concerned we were becoming good friends. As far as I was concerned we were becoming more than just good friends, even if I had to make her wake up to herself and see the fact. Did I mention that she is gorgeous?

Our lunchtimes were passing by effortlessly. They had become the highlight of my day. I had heard about girls like Ellie Parker. She could be my best pal and girl-friend at the same time. I just had to get her to agree to the girlfriend bit. One lunchtime, she slipped into the conversation that her parents were away. So I thought, this is it! This is my chance to be romantic! It does not come naturally, but I will do my best. I rode over to her place that night on my tiny two-stroke motorbike. When it went up hills it sounded like a lawnmower that had hit a particularly thick tuft of grass. I knew that she would be able to hear me coming from a mile off so when I got to the top of her hill I hit the kill switch and rolled down in neutral to evade detection. (That sounds suss. My intentions were honourable.) When I got to her place I threw stones on her balcony until she emerged from her bed. She looked like a stunned possum, big green eyes peeping over the balcony. 'Ellie, it's me! Don't freak out!' 'Tom what are you doing here?' 'I thought I might visit. I've brought a joint.' That Wednesday night we stayed up late. We played hide-and-seek for what seemed like hours but was probably only ten minutes and laughed ourselves silly until we kissed. I was just excited to have our faces close together, let alone to be kissing. Wow.

When I saw Ellie Parker the next day at uni it was after I had just come off stage from winning the university stand-up comedy competition. I had found my muse. I had found my love. I asked Ellie Parker to be my girlfriend. She said, 'Why?' I said, 'Because we could hang out with each other every day for the rest of our lives and not get bored.' We argued about this for a while because she likes to be contrary. Then she said she might as well be my girlfriend. Not quite what I had planned, but near enough's good enough.

Ellie Parker had always told me that when she finished university she was going on a trip to Italy. It was her passion. She had been there when she was sixteen and it had changed her life. She had always planned to return and this plan did not include me. I met her in first year so this trip to Italy was always ages away. But when the time finally came it hit me like a sneaky punch to the stomach. By this stage I had long since finished university and had been a stand-up comic for years, travelling and leaving Ellie Parker at home to imagine how much fun I was having. This was her chance to exact revenge. 'I'm going to Italy for six months, maybe longer. I don't know when

I'm coming back.' Yeah, no worries. I will just chill out back here and write a few emails. SIX FUCKING MONTHS! The longest I had ever been away on tour was nine weeks, and even then I came back for a visit in the middle. Ellie reminded me that if I added up all the times that I had been touring it equalled more than six months so we were even. And besides, Ellie Parker had been planning on taking this trip before she met me six years earlier. She said I could come over and visit her for Christmas in the middle of her trip, which softened the blow – but still, six fucking months.

Ellie and I fell further in love. The kind of love where we had so many in-jokes that we did not even speak English any more to each other. We were living together by then which had only made us closer and happier. In the nights leading up to her departure we were getting along so well that we would go to sleep laughing in each other's faces. Why were we doing this to ourselves? There were tears at the airport.

In a weird twist of fate I moved cities for work just as she moved countries for leisure. For the first few weeks that Ellie was away I did not actually miss her that much. We talked on the phone, emailed each other and got by. In fact, I was enjoying living alone. I felt overwhelming relief that once the house was tidied up it would stay that way. Ellie and I defy gender stereotypes. I am tidy. She is messy. She forces me to use phrases such as 'Can you pick up your clothes please?' and 'Can you not throw flour on the carpet?' When I finish cleaning the kitchen I see completeness and calm. When Ellie sees a clean kitchen she sees an opportunity to bake. When I see Ellie baking I see an opportunity to clean up again.

So with Ellie away I went about my tidy life. Doing what I wanted to do when I wanted to do it. Then I realised something. Life is pretty miserable if you have no one to share it with. This reminded me of my dad. My dad was a farmer. When he was a young man just starting out, his parents went away for the weekend. Dad found himself on his own. He thought, this is what it must be like for Uncle Martin who lives out on his farm by himself. What a bloody miserable existence. So Dad decided right then that he would get busy getting married and having a family. Suddenly I had an idea. Ellie and I should get married. What a brilliant idea! Ellie loves Italy. I can propose to her when I visit her at Christmas. What about on New Year's Eve? Brilliant! That is even better! I was doing a little that-was-a-brilliant-idea dance in my head. We will count in the New Year together and I will pop the question! I have never done anything that romantic in my life ever. This will blow her away. I have got a job to do.

I became obsessed. Instead of wasting my time missing Ellie I put all that energy into making plans. I say plans but there was not much to do. Buy ring. Propose. I thought I would ask her parents' permission. I get on well with Ellie's parents so this was not too big a deal. We went out to dinner and I asked them if I could marry their daughter. Ellie's father thought it was a good idea. Ellie's mother wanted to know what I would do if she said no. I said, 'As if she would say no. I'm only going to ask because I know that she will say yes. The fun bit is that Ellie would never expect a cynic like me to propose in the first place.' Ellie's mother said that Ellie always said from a young age that she did not want to get married. I knew this. Ellie always talked about how she did not want to get married, but at the same time she loved weddings. Ellie also said that Valentine's Day was sappy, but if you gave her a bunch of flowers she would melt.

One thing that had always intrigued me about engagement rings is the cost. Some people say you are supposed to spend one month's salary. I am a comedian. What if that month included a television show, five corporate events and a commercial? Off to Tiffany's for me. What if that month included waiting at home by the phone? Off to Cash Converters for me. My decision was made easy. Ellie hates diamonds and her mother assured me that a designer friend of hers had made a ring that Ellie was in love with. So I thought, however much it costs I will get it. And get it I did. 'How much?' I hear you asking. None of your business. Let us just say it was somewhere between Tiffany's and Cash Converters. I popped the ring in my bag and got ready for my trip to Italy.

In another weird twist, on my last day in Australia my house got broken into. This was about three days before Christmas. The front door was smashed. My laptop was nicked. My video camera was nicked. My engagement ring was not nicked. I do not know why. Maybe it was a romantic junkie that broke in. Whoever it was they were like a reverse Santa Claus. Just before Christmas they smashed through the front door instead of the chimney, removed my presents and then nicked off to steal presents from all the other children in the neighbourhood. I do not know why this is important to the story but it just meant that I went off to Italy with a feeling of unease. I was nervous about the proposal, and now I also felt weird about my home not being the same when I returned.

Once I was on the plane my anxiety about the break-in gave way to daydreams about my adventure. Ellie and I were going to spend Christmas with her parents in Rome and from there we were going to head off on our own to Venice. New Year's Eve, Venice and the ring that she had fallen in love with. It was too easy. The nerves were giving way to smugness.

When I first saw Ellie in Italy it was outside our hotel in Rome. She was four months into her blissful journey and I was one day later from having my house broken into. Our stress levels were not quite matched in that I was stressed and she was not. When we first went to kiss she kissed me on the cheek. This would have broken the heart of any man who had not seen their future fiancée in over four months, but this is Ellie we are talking about. Ellie is very absentminded. She gets left and right mixed up, under and over confused, lips and cheek the wrong way around. Often she forgets and kisses me on the cheek after she has been greeting friends. This is a problem that continues on to today. To the point that whenever we meet I announce 'Lips'. (The other side of the coin is that once I accidentally kissed a male friend of mine goodbye on the mouth. Considering I do not kiss any men this is quite a mistake.) So I announced to Ellie, 'Lips,' and we kissed and everyone lived happily ever after.

In the middle of the Australian summer I had come to the middle of the European winter. Jet lag, shock to my thermostat and the fact that as a tall man the Old World did not fit me made me feel very uncomfortable. All the doorways were too low in Rome. I spent Christmas in an apartment, half of which I could not stand up in. Here I was, ready to tell a woman that we fit together, in a country that I did not fit in. Italy surprised me in many ways. First of all I could not believe how much Italians love Italy and Italian food. There were only Italian restaurants. Doesn't anyone eat a curry ever? I felt like whispering in every second Italian's ear, 'It turns out Thai food is quite yum!' Another thing that surprised me was that Italy has its very own bogans. I always thought of Italians as being very stylish – well it turns out that some of them are not. Seeing badly dressed Italians reminded me of when I saw my first unfunny English comedian or when I saw a black American singing out of tune. It made me feel great!

Christmas, to be fair, was a bit of a trial for me. Ellie is an only child so staying with her and her parents meant I was staying with a complete family. Families have their own shorthand and despite all the best intentions it is easy to feel left out. Also, you always feel like you are fitting in with other people's plans. 'Let's all meet for lunch at 1 pm.' 'How about we get hungry first?' 'All right, let's get hungry after we visit the museum at 11.15 am.' So although I love Ellie's parents dearly, it was a relief when they left because it meant that Ellie and I could start our holiday together.

We started our beautiful holiday, in an extravagant, marble-floored apartment that overlooked the Piazza Navona, by watching videos. There is a guilty pleasure in wasting time when you are overseas. Sometimes you just want to bunk in. The apartment we were staying in had two videos: *The Deer Hunter* and *The Thin Red Line*. What kind of intense dude did this apartment belong to? 'I just want to have two films, that's it. I want them both to be about war but I want them to be intellectual.' We watched these films back to back. We were shattered but it brought us closer together. For the rest of our trip we were making jokes about some intense dude who travels to Rome once a year, watches those two films, then flies home. It was clearly time to get out of Rome.

Ellie had booked accommodation in Venice but we had two nights that we had not booked for. New Year's Eve and the first of January. No problem, let's find some accommodation on New Year's Eve in Venice. Oh, hang on. Everything is booked out, what a surprise. Ellie came up with an ingenious plan. Why don't we stay somewhere regional, off the tourist trail, on the way to Venice? So we booked two nights in an old nunnery in Assisi. That was that. I would propose to Ellie in Assisi.

Assisi is gorgeous. It is a medieval town perched on a hill in the middle of a farming area. I grew up on a farm in Australia so this is weird to me. Regional areas and history do not go together. The primary school where I grew up was just over a hundred years old and that was the oldest thing I knew. The nunnery we were staying in was older than European settlement in Australia. Here we were in Assisi, surrounded by similar farming land to where I grew up, but there were cobblestone roads, a wall fortifying the town and a cathedral where St Francis was buried in the thirteenth century.

That afternoon while we were walking the streets I thought I heard a gunshot really close to us. Ellie and I jumped in our skins. I was already on edge because tonight was the big night. We looked around to see an old Italian man laughing at us and tiny bits of red paper everywhere. The same tiny bits of red paper that I remember having seen in the sink in the science lab at my school after my friend Luke had dropped a bunger into it. Loose firecracker laws and New Year's Eve – what a great combination! As the afternoon turned to evening the frequency of these gunshots increased. They were deafening as they echoed down the narrow medieval streets. Every time we heard a bang Ellie and I laughed. Tulips are Ellie's favourite flowers. She loves the way that after they have opened up too much they look like they have exploded. So every time we heard an explosion that night we would comment 'Tulips anyone?' And then laugh hysterically at our own little in-joke that no one had any possibility of understanding.

Ellie and I tried to book a restaurant for the night but everything was booked out. We ended up getting a table for a 10 pm sitting at a fairly average restaurant, no different to if a crappy Norton Street restaurant had been picked up and dumped in Assisi. I was starting to get really nervous. It was tonight! I had Ellie's favourite ring in my pocket. I was dressed up nicely, wearing a fancy leather jacket I had bought in Rome. The atmosphere was perfect.

After an average dinner of, for something different, pasta, we headed to the town square where a local band was playing. They sang standard covers in English but the between-song banter was in Italian, to which Ellie would laugh and I would be bamboozled. To get through these moments of being left out of a joke, I would just imagine tulips exploding to cheer me up. I kept checking my watch. It was fast approaching midnight. My heart was starting to thump. I had loved Ellie for over six years. We were best mates. We knew each other inside out. But in this moment I felt like we had just met for the first time. I had a whole butterfly enclosure in my stomach making me tremble. I have performed stand-up comedy on live television knowing that over a million people are suddenly going to find me funny or not and my heart has not skipped a beat. At this moment a nifty TV spot would have been a lot easier to cope with.

Ten, nine, eight, seven, hold Ellie, six, five, grab the ring, four, three, get ready, two, set, one, go.

'Ellie, will you marry me?' I have a very loud voice but

this question came out a lot quieter than I had planned. Ellie was staring at me with her big green eyes. All around us everyone was cheering Happy New Year or whatever the Italian version is for that.

'I don't know what to say,' Ellie said.

'Yes or no?' I prompted her. She was in shock. She had not seen it coming.

'I can't say yes.'

Okay. No worries. Now not only did I feel like I had just met her for the first time, I felt like I had just proposed to someone I had met for the first time who had said no because it was a preposterous idea. I now felt like I was holding the neighbour's cat too tightly and it clearly wanted to run off. Ellie burst into tears, which was a rip-off because I was pretty sure it was me who had just had their feelings hurt. We went straight back to our hotel room, crying all the way. How could two best mates have got it so wrong?

As we were walking back, even though I was dizzy with a pain I had never known in my life, I still remember looking across the plains of Assisi and seeing every little village lit up by chaotic fireworks. None of those organised, safety first, highly choreographed Harbour Bridge pieces of crap. It was one of the most beautiful sights of my trip mismatched with the most disappointing emotion. Anyway, chin up. We still had a week's holiday to enjoy in Venice, the city for lovers. This trip would have worked out so much better if she had said yes.

We cried all night and when we woke up we must have been really traumatised because we went for a jog. We never jog. Italians do not jog. We looked like Americans. The next night we kept talking around in circles.

'If you don't want to marry me, why don't you break up with me?'

'Because I love you.'

'But if you loved me, you would have said yes.'

'I can't say yes.'

'If you can't say yes to spending the rest of your life with me, we should break up.'

'But I love you.'

'But if you loved me, you would have said yes.'

'But I can't say yes.'

'If you can't say yes, we should break up.'

'But I love you.'

'But if you loved me, you would have said yes.'

'Do you want to go for a jog?'

'Yes.'

Ellie and I worked out that no decision could be reached. So we would just have to work it out when Ellie got back to Australia a couple of months after me. We would make the most of our trip to Venice. We must have been really traumatised because we both took up smoking. Ellie hates smoking so this was especially weird. I do not remember that much about our week in Venice. I remember that the heating in our hotel room was so hot that we had to leave a window open even though it was snowing outside. I remember being disturbed by the fact that the high tide filled the Piazza San Marco with the ocean and the locals just put down duckboards and got on with their lives. I remember buying a pizza and paying for it in coins to get rid of all my change, only to have a German tourist say to me, 'Is zat ze last of your monies?' And then fall about laughing for a disturbingly rude length of time. I do not remember how we got through that week given that our relationship had changed forever.

When I got back to Australia it seemed that everyone I had ever known was getting married. A friend from work had even been to Italy and proposed while over there. I remember him saying, 'I'm glad she said yes because if she had said no it would have been a pretty miserable holiday.' I nodded in agreement while a tiny voice inside me said 'Ouch!' Someone even asked me, 'You were in Italy, did you pop the question?' I said no. I do not like people feeling sorry for me. What was I going to say? 'Yeah, I asked Ellie to marry me but she said no. We are still together though. She gets home in another month or two. I actually don't know when she is getting home. So, yeah, I couldn't be happier.'

When Ellie finally did get back to Australia we moved back in together in a new city. Moving in together to resolve your problems is supposed to be a no-no but it worked for us. We finally came to this conclusion: 'Will you marry me?' was the right question but at the wrong time. Ellie was in the middle of an adventure feeling free and there I was trying to tie her down. We might get married one day, who knows? We have agreed that I can ask the question or she can too. I am going away for two months to the UK soon. Maybe she can visit me while I am over there and propose to me. Would I say yes or would it be too spitefully delicious to say no?

I would say yes.

I have not told any of my family or friends this story. I do not know why. At the time I felt too humiliated. Now that time has passed it is too much bother to explain it to them just out of the blue. So now if they ask me the annoying, commonly asked question, 'Why aren't you two married yet?' I will give them a copy of this book and say, 'Read this and don't ask me that question ever again.'

Letters to a Faraway Land

EMILY BALLOU

The two figures who had come into being through all this passing back and forth of sheets of paper, however close they came to what was most real in them, existed on a level of language that could not, he thought, be translated into ordinary discourse, and would shrink back, to hover as ghostly onlookers, from a world whose familiar scenes and habits, whose many reminders of previous occasions, old awkwardnesses and affections, judgements, errors, would inevitably call back their heavier, more ordinary selves.

– David Malouf, *Conversations at Curlow Creek*

I love you. That is all I know. But all I know, too, is that
I am writing into space: the kind of dreadful, unknown
space I am just going to enter. I am going to Iowa,
Illinois, Idaho, Indindiana, but these, though mis-spelt,
are on the map. You are not.

– Dylan Thomas in a letter to his wife, Caitlin

I was writing when I met him. If our relationship was a
map, it was coded in the moment we first spoke, my hand
hovering above the half-scribbled page. It was as if I had
been waiting all my life at that table, writing, until he
found me. That journal entry ended abruptly. Outside it
had been snowing, thick flakes that had covered me; that
had stuck to my eyelashes, soaked my coat. I looked up
from the table in the cafeteria and he was there, saying
something – what was it he was saying? I could only hear
his accent. He asked my name.

What is a name to such a meeting? I might as well
have introduced myself as America, and he as Australia,
for those placenames would overwhelm any other name
we had already been given and any we would subse-
quently give each other. Those words were the first and
most important marks in the cartography of our love. We
were countries about to form a coalition. It was spelled
out from the first second we spoke; each was a tabula
rasa for the other's romantic projections. Boy with accent
spelled instant passport to unknown lands. Girl with pen
in hand spelled potential spoils for adventuring to foreign
shores. I am not meaning to be cynical about the meeting

that would entirely transform my future life, but I can't – even when handing over the writing to my twenty-one-year-old self who knew better than I now do exactly what happened – pretend there isn't always some sort of impossible agenda at stake when those who were born on opposite sides of the world first meet. Even if the intention is a bit of traveller's fun – sex without strings – all the big issues that in other relationships take time to come to the fore are played out, although perhaps unspoken, within the first few minutes. Either we will fuck for a bit and then never see each other again or we will sign up for a lifetime of geographical schizophrenia. There are no easy wins in this hand that we are sure fate has dealt us. (But what exploration is suddenly possible too. What a heart-pounding troubadourean trip . . .)

We were apart from the moment we met; very quickly, there was this sense of unrealisable longing; there were the usual uncertainties and impossible distances to be crossed, emotional at first, and then geographical. I was twenty-one and in love with several people – obsessed in my journals with three 'boys', as I called them. Jonathan was the unlucky third, though he stood out from the others for being the only one who could take me away from the suffocation of my tiny world, and the only one, I suspected, who actually loved me. I never felt I'd been loved back before, had never had a 'real relationship' (defined back then according to whether the other's intensity was as obsessive as my own), yet in a typical twenty-one-year-old way I was also wary of anything that felt too good.

After only knowing him for a month he invited me on a road trip to Toronto, where he would apply for a visa to work in the States. I still wasn't sure then how I felt about him. Though I was charmed by his accent, his exotic childhood, raised half in Singapore, half in Australia, his reckless romantic bravery, and his intense blue eyes, I was keeping my distance, scared of what love with this faraway, near-stranger might mean.

We drove twelve hours, sometimes talking, sometimes silent, listening to Leonard Cohen and Cowboy Junkies, watching the edge of Canada form on the horizon, the United States receding with the sun. We crossed the border and left our passports on the line; we passed through to new selves, a new time, without origins. There, in a country where neither of us had been born, could we make a space of our own?

We stayed in a grandmothery guest house, a tiny room with a crocheted doona cover and faded flower prints on the walls. I heard him squeak in the bathtub as he washed himself. I didn't know him really at all, but he was becoming my companion of unfamiliar parts – lands and hearts. The next day we sat drinking coffee and writing in a café – facing each other, spilling thoughts onto the page, doing in person what we would end up doing for years, as though the width of a table were no different to the span of a globe. A rush of unfamiliar faces passed the windows. People crept in, wet, smelling of rain. Our hands across the table, sharing greasy, crunchy fries, brushing past each other, told nothing of the way we'd held each other all night as if we would otherwise dissolve. Or how when he touched me, I cried.

I remember best, from those early days, lying on various floors and beds with him, his big eyes watching me; and holding myself back from him, changing clothes in the closet out of shyness. I would hear him giggle from the bed, protesting, 'But Em, I've already felt and seen your entire body . . .' but still to the closet I went, like a ritual, like a good American girl. I didn't know how to be a body with another person. I didn't know how to put my face next to another, or how to breathe with them breathing beside me all night, his arm clasping the belly I hated. I had never been so intensely watched before and I found myself both shrinking and swelling under his gaze. When he talked to me, looked at me, touched me, I felt real for the first time in my life.

We were together long enough – two months perhaps – to feel ourselves in love and then go our separate ways, without really knowing if we would meet again. We played then in a torturous realm (*nothing* would ever bring us back together; I would *never* see him again; the whole affair had been a big *lie*).

Jonathan left today. Our goodbye was all wrong. Outside, grey-blue skies before rain – skies the colour of house paint, thick and hazy. I want to be touched by rough wetness and wind. I want to be blown down the block like a newspaper, an empty useless thing. There are tears on the window. Like last night down my face when I thought of you, touching me.

I can read my journals from that time. I can read the letters and the flood of longing that rises from the paper – hundreds of sheets of tiny handwriting, mine on ragged-edged pages ripped from my journal, his on nearly translucent soft stationery, folded into tiny white squares, in white envelopes, marked with faraway postmarks. The first letters are tentative – we felt our way into each other's lives by degrees – then suddenly, impercept-ibly, the paper starts to burn. And it's hard to look back on my younger self, to read, as if an outsider, the pining of my barely adult heart and allow it to still be mine, to allow it its place in my trajectory of self; to know that without its sometimes melodramatic desires, I would not now be here.

I can read from them now – like a conversation between two selves, one older, perhaps wiser, and one younger and certainly less cynical – how passion is always a question of tense, most real in the present moment. Like pain, it cannot precisely be remembered. I can read the way love letters come into existence from a soul to a soul in duplicate, one copy forming inside me, while its facsimile, as if meticulously inked by a medieval scribe, appears inside my lover as he reads it back: marginalia of the heart. I can read too how love fades, will fade always if not maintained; but how it grows again in the shape of a new face. And each face is as faraway from me as the last was, as the next one will be.

Have you really not noticed, then, that here of all places, in this private personal solitude that surrounds me, I have turned to you?

– Gustave Flaubert to his mistress, Louise Colet

The words have always been there. Like a well I keep full until the drought, like a bank account I keep depositing into, the stores of love's language lie waiting for a chance to be used.

Today, I might use my pen or my voice, but once upon a time, they were the same thing.

Alberto Manguel wrote: 'Augustine . . . knew that letters . . . were "signs [or 'sighs' as I mis-read it] of sounds" . . . The written text was a conversation, put on paper so that the absent partner would be able to pronounce the words intended for him.' During the great era of the repressed romantic, the nineteenth century, the letter became a secret intimacy acceptable only between those who were engaged. It allowed all that could not otherwise be said in person to be privately uttered. So a letter was an alternative to a live presence, a precursor to the telephone's transported spoken voice, an 'aural hallucination', as Manguel named it, and also the most secret text of that voice, transported in a golden-wafer wrapping mere tongues and throats could never conjure. Thin as it is, capable of slipping between a lover's lips like the slot on a mailbox, a letter is a house for the soul. It is the *sigh* of that soul.

Is that why, even now, when voicemail, mobile, text, email, and 24-hour CNN coverage provides all we might ever desire of 'live', the love letter still breathes hotly – endangered as it may be – from its paper shell? Is this why we still take that small folded square into our hands like a precious bar of gold?

Jonathan travelled out East to teach drama at a summer camp for rich kids. I was left, living between my mother's, several friends' houses and my car so I could save money, wandering the streets of absent love.

It seems so strange to try to remember you as much as I want to. Your smell, the realness of you I've forgotten. Though I love even my gauzy memory of you . . . When I see you, you will look changed somehow, will be changed, as I will be, and I'll have to stare at you strangely until I remember your face. It's scary how quickly it vanishes, even as it beats in my heart and mind and in photos all around me.

We wrote letters; we waited for letters (*our two embracing mailboxes*); we pined; we made and waited for phone calls. There was a problem with his paycheque at first, so I sent him money in envelopes just so he could call me, then sat at a friend's house, by the phone, dressed to impress, waiting for it to ring, aesthetically prepared to step into the role of *lover* the second it sounded; spent nights drunk in love's rags when it didn't. I dreamed love and all the things love would say to the lover, but woke alone, sweating in July's stink, stuck to the back seat of my car. I pulled pages of his pale translucent heart from the floor. I dozed with his photo in my fingers, trying to hang on to fading things.

At the end of that summer, I drove across the country in my little white Subaru to find him sunny and brown, in his sandshoes, flipping back his floppy hair to reveal those deep blue eyes that wouldn't stop grinning at me.

We spent the night in his friend's house, in a room where we were told a boa constrictor was on the loose, but that did not stop us from falling naked onto every soft coil of warmth in that dark space of four walls, our fingers moving like snakes across skin, slowly feeling and swallowing everything that we were sure had been eternally snatched from us.

We went camping at Cape Cod, in Massachusetts, to the dunes. We took photos of each other in order to memorise the rich infinity of the other's face. We unfurled stories from childhood like wings.

But soon, lying in the tent, rain and sun and birdsong taking turns splattering against our nylon home, I began exhibiting the first signs of a new existential fever. When Jonathan had been away there was waiting and writing. I felt myself plummeting. I thought I'd *die* of longing. *What* was *my self without him? Would I be loved? What exactly did love mean between two people who never actually saw each other? And whatever it was, could it last?* Then, in the moment of reunion, when the agony of waiting ceased (and conversely I felt myself about to *die* of happiness) so did all writing. I was *reunited*, but strangely felt myself clawed apart, in pieces. Again, plummeting. I found myself unable to *do* anything. I existed only as a creature, pre-linguistic, nine parts love. This creature's daily life: have sex, wake up, have sex, gurgle in amorous dialects, have a wee, go back to sleep, have sex, eat something, hug, babble incoherent intensities, have sex, get dressed, get undressed, hug, have sex, sleep . . . We lived in only the smallest spaces: the car, the tent, a circle of arms, trailing wet towels and sand from the dunes back into our bed.

There was separateness – intense, overwhelming absence – and then there was reunion – intense, over-whelming presence. Could we find a balance between them?

> . . . *the way you will fly home soon*
> *in the afternoon on Sunday, six days*
> *I could see it in your face*
> *how the light from other places*
> *criss-crossed in black*
> *welts and you were shadowed*
> *my fingers whips*
> *when all I wanted*
> *was to hold your face.*

I didn't want to ponder this question however, much less ask it, because for now we were destined to seesaw the extremes. Jonathan was going back to Australia in a few days.

In my dream you left me, but on the phone we moved through time zones, through the Arctic, the tundra, the deserts, the oceans, wind, temperature, climate, days, islands, the ice ages; from my cool October autumn leaves to your warm spring Sunday morning and you . . . where are you? You seem so far away now and we no longer share nights and days; we never see the moon at the same time . . .

My fingers learned the twelve digits that would take me to him, one for each thousand miles of telephone wire we had to cross. Somewhere his name was shouted. I was left dangling.

'Hi . . .' (No words can express the sound of this smiling voice after a hungry week – part whisper, part honey, slow and sweet.)

'Hiiiiii . . .'

The telephone. What a troublesome technology in the face of love. There is no face, and yet, my imagination can conjure it; his voice can whisper like a ghost in my ear. I can lie on my bed with my feet up the wall and close my eyes and listen to this voice – its melodies, changes in cadence, rhythm – talking to me in a way it never talks to me, except in bed. Its poetry is breath. So close that it cuts straight into the innermost whorl of my ear.

'Hey you . . .'

But I could not see him. Perhaps after all, he really was just a myth, a ghostly figment of my desire-weary imagination; a stranger on the other side of the world I'd happened to call accidentally, like a child playing pranks and punching in random numbers.

'So hi . . .'

There was an awkward pause, followed by an echo of that awkward pause inching down the line. Everything we said all wrong to each other was played back to us at a dollar a minute, my own voice as strange as his, foreign and unreachable, each utterance casting forth double doses of romantic humiliation.

'Hello?' *Hello?* I was a girl on the edge of a cliff and I was calling into the silence and hearing myself louder than the wind. I couldn't seem to find the words that would lead me back to him.

'Yeah, I'm still here . . .' *Still here . . .*

No, you are not. You are not here and you do not even seem to be there. There is nowhere we exist together.

This is the difference between flying and falling.

'Did you just wake up?'

'Mm-hmm. I'm standing here in my underwear, shivering . . .'

'I'm sorry.'

'Hey, it's . . . don't apologise. I'm happy shivering in my underwear.'

'Well, ah,' my voice falling into a whisper, although I was alone. 'I . . . just wanted . . . need to tell you that, ah, my period didn't come . . .'

'Really?' He sounded slightly excited.

'I'm serious, I'm *really* worried, Jonathan . . .'

Worried especially that all of our beautiful desperately-in-love-letters had been some sort of narcissistic performance; a drama of a passion that will not survive.

'Oh Em, don't worry! You're not pregnant! Or are you?' Still excited.

'Don't say that so loud.'

'It's okay, my mum doesn't care.'

'Your *mom* is there?!'

'Well not just my mum, my family. They're having breakfast.'

'Where are you?'

'In the kitchen.'

'In your underwear?!'

'So? I told you, I was sleeping.'

'You just said the word *pregnant* while talking to me . . . in front of your family?!' I could barely say the words – I was whispering for the both of us.

'Sweetie, calm down, stop worrying! My family's reading the paper.'

'I bet they're just pretending to read the paper now! I'm sure they're all tuned right in. I can't believe you're talking to me about this in front of your mom. In your underwear. I'm so embarrassed.'

He giggled. 'Oh Em, don't be such a Yank.'

I might have taken from this conversation something more than his worrying excitement that, at twenty-one, I was potentially the mother of his child. All the things, both beautiful and not, about the differences between America and Australia, him and I, travelled that thin telephone wire. Relaxed openness, emotional transparency and a circle of family, adult family who still chose to eat together.

I was not pregnant in the end. But something was nevertheless born on the crossed lines of our love. His family in the happy kitchen, eating breakfast around the table: how much I now love them.

I wonder if Alexander Bell, the product of a deaf mother and a father determined to rid the world of stam-

mering, had any inkling of what an eloquent yet frustrat-
ingly stone-deaf device he had invented. Phone home,
phone for heartbreak, phone for good love – but be
prepared to pay a toll. How many times had I received a
beautiful letter from Jonathan – a letter that I could read
again and again, confirmation that I was loved in the
most understood and essential way – only to have it
followed up by a phone call in which nothing essential
could be expressed, no common ground reached. The
letter said everything; the phone call said nothing but 'I
don't know how to reach you.' In the silence of that
reverberating line I secretly say, *I love you I love you I
love you*, but I hang up, sure that all my lover heard in
that silence was: *I really couldn't be bothered having a
decent conversation with you.*

The letter speaks an eternal present – *I am waiting* –
that delicately holds both the past (from which the letter
was actually written) and the future (in which the letter
will be received) in a perfect balance. Those rare modern-
day letter writers and receivers also benefit from the
historical romantic register of the letter, where everything
that is suffered is suffered *in extremis*, making the person
we can't touch or smell or see more perfectly rendered in
their agonising absence. This absence is rather desirable,
most necessary, for it causes such goodwill to pulse
through our hearts. And what is as pleasurable (besides
that first cup of tea in the morning) as the tremors of
acute and perfect longing? The phone call, on the other
hand, in its fumbling imperfections, its broken dialogue,

is in turns both eternal and too quick to end, denying both the past and the future simultaneously:

Whatever love we had before this phone call is now gone.

Whatever love we might have in the future, after this phone call, will be impossible.

You and I will never understand each other.

Jonathan and I hung up, as we often did, dispirited, empty, a hollow receiver to our ear with the dial tone ringing out. The other was gone.

We each returned to our lives and to our desks to compose yet another letter in which our longing was more perfectly captured; in which we imagined we were whole again.

I just got off the phone with you – also poisoned, with you, your voice, your sweet words. You make me both happy and intensely frustrated. You certainly have your way with moods, as I do. What do I always say that is wrong? My words are never enough, my love and my kissing are never enough. I think that you yearn so deeply for something. Perhaps part of what you want is that yearning – you will never be satisfied because it is the search as much as the result that drives you. Do you think? I am that way too. The drive the search the wait. I am insatiable, I guess. We both are – driven together in the inexhaustible search . . . will we find what we are looking for?

We are thus far separated – but after all one mile is as

bad as a thousand – which is a great consolation to
one who must travel six hundred before he meets you
again . . .

          – Lord Byron to his wife, Annabella Milbanke

I have told my tale of arrival in this country so often, and
in so many ways, that it has become a bit like my own
personal dreamtime, my story of origins; as if I came into
existence only the moment that Qantas jet touched down;
as if before that time, I had merely been embryonic,
waiting to begin.

I had rehearsed this new beginning in my letters to
Jonathan – letters to a future in which I charted a new
course for the self. Over four long months I sat waiting
in a window over a cobblestone Milwaukee street *(I am
marking days off on my calendar . . . I want to light
candles and burn out the loneliness . . .)*, watching the
steam rise from a manhole and the autumn wheel down,
while Jonathan scrubbed and painted in fresh spring heat
to turn a Pyrmont workers cottage into a home for us.
Writing became a way for me to practise love, and simultaneously, love became an interesting new way to practise
writing. *Our love is so exciting, so new in our letters,
because we can say whatever we need to, however we
want, in as much time as it takes to say it. And of course
for me, writing is essential – so for you to know that side
of me is as important as knowing my body or my
soul . . . And I will miss this letter-writing when I get
there.* We wrote in order to practise who we were, who

we might be together, the people we would become. That person I would become, I hoped, was also a writer.

We were twenty-two. All was still new. All was up for grabs.

It's hard to remember now what I knew really, before I came here, about the climate, the topography of Australia, what I knew about myself even. But what I certainly didn't know was the way the landscape, this land I now live inside, would become a new road through my heart, cut, as I imagine any new road must be, with pick-axe-hard work and sledgehammers and bulldozers and sweat. At the end of it, there is a path through what was once impassable rock, and I do not notice at first, all the golden quartz of the sandstone crumbled around me in the dust. I only discover its broken shimmer later; I will find bits of it sticking to my skin, catching the light. I realise that, like quartz – which, with its diamond-scratching strength, never actually breaks down, just remakes itself into new forms – what I thought was completely shattered in the making of the map of my new life remained there all this time.

Fifteen years later, I can bend down, I can press my fingers to the ground and bring it up, stuck to my skin: gold. The smallest fragments of self.

Like quartz, the crystals of self re-form with each new subsequent love, becoming here a beach, here a chunk of sandstone with a river of iron-rust running through it, before ending up as the cornerstone of a house hand-chiselled from the side of a hill. But still rain and wind and frost and snow will break it down again, and time, and salt, and fickle hearts too.

In December of 1990, I arrived in Australia for the first time: me, my notebook and my fickle heart.

I love, I love, I love . . .

Of course there was the daze, the haze of landing here – halfway around the world, to fall into the arms of this boy I loved and had missed so desperately. There was the sudden freedom of that love, the feeling that we had a year to ourselves, to find out what this love might be. There were no plunging jerking dreams of lovers snatched and planes missed and phone lines disconnected, dreams of arrivals in which Jonathan refused to kiss me.

There was the freedom to slow down, to spend days in bed.

There was of course the dazzle of light I found here, and a sky a size never before seen. There was my brash, loud boot-stomping American self, walking from our sweet little cottage on Union Street, across the Pyrmont Bridge, through the city, up Oxford Street to the College of Fine Arts, where I was studying: a sweet, small campus tucked like a nest inside the reaching branches of great, old Moreton Bay fig trees. There was the strangeness of new customs. There was a new family and unfamiliar foods, the usual accumulation of firsts and never-befores, the great cultural landslide; the beautiful and frightening feeling of being absolutely without moorings. The Gulf War was imminent. The unfamiliarity and fun of experiencing a hot New Year's was overshadowed by the explosive echoes of the fireworks over the Harbour Bridge, which only conjured the sounds of war. Jonathan's family took me to Bali for a month and we spent the entire Gulf War huddled over a crackling radio tuned to the BBC, on a rain-splattered patio tiled with tiny hopping frogs.

Back in Sydney, Jonathan and I slept. All day sometimes, as though love was too heavy to hold us, as though the weight of the burden we placed on it tugged at our soles, threatened to yank us down, down, into an unconscious, warm, pre-natal sleep.

We just had a fight. One minute we are so happy, romping around the bed drenched in sweat and breathless and then naked, we lay together talking and then whoosh – I am so sad, this incredible sadness that wants to split me. I think I have been too lazy here, wrapped up in sleep. How do we sleep? All day? We tie ourselves together. I am using up all my energy trying to get inside him – I drain myself . . . Right now I don't know where I want to be. I want to be here – I want to be away, alone. But how can I leave these arms, this love? Is it possible to be a whole woman – a woman, a writer, a beautiful loved woman who is smart, who is emotional? . . . I must not let myself be drained. I must demand my own time –

*I must demand me – apart from him. I must demand a
break from all this winding, twisting, kissing . . .*

It's hard not to judge this relationship now, fourteen
years on – not to look back and say, in a superior, thera-
peutic kind of way, 'Well, clearly, there were some issues
here.' It wasn't just the added pressure of distance, of
being in a relationship that without modern transport
would never have been possible, that required one or the
other lover to pick up their life and watch it land,
awkwardly, in the dirt on the other side of the world, to
find it didn't really fit within any allocated spaces, or that
the colours were garish, all wrong.

Nor was it simply the extra strong dose of isolation,
separation from my family, friends and support, from the
sense of inhabiting a familiar life. All that I'd been so
quick to jettison in favour of my *becoming*, were the very
things that had previously given me my only real sense of
belonging.

And while all of these complications were certainly
difficult, they were compounded by the very terms of our
meeting, and by the terms of romantic love itself. The
things that made us fall in love were necessarily also what
prevented our relationship from thriving long-term.
Longing was predicated on our hardly knowing each
other, on being quickly whisked away from each other's
sight and grasp, and on cultivating desire over several
intense months inside the space of our own heads. We
expanded with romance, but crucially, we also expanded
in the knowledge that *we were loved*. Such a relationship,

built on geographical separateness, can hardly survive the subsequent, constant togetherness, because what I loved about him from a distance; and what he loved best in me, was that we had let love breathe.

Of course there is always the very real, though obvious, difference between longing and having. But what relationship, forever oscillating between the two, can withstand such heat?

It is so quiet here. Jonathan is working later than I thought. This is my life – this book, this empty place, my typewriter. Wrote no letters today. Came home angry but my fingers were too cold to type and I had no energy. Instead I cried. I wanted tonight to write about happy things, observe. Instead of moon, there are tears and holes and awful silences. The fridge hums, my eyes droop. There is no reason for me to continue in this way, but what other way would I continue? What is my life here without Jonathan? It is hard to go from a place where everyone loves you to one where nobody even knows you, much less loves you.

My early journals from when I first lived in Australia expressed much anxiety about how to marry my writing soul with the soul of another. How did one love *and* write? I felt it was an impossible combination, and it was an issue that flared as soon as the loved one and I were reunited. As Oscar Wilde wrote bitterly in 'De Profundis', the letter he wrote to his once-lover Lord Alfred Douglas from the exile of Reading Gaol: 'During the whole time we were together I never wrote one single line.'

In the absence of our love letters, my journal became my place of words, and since journalling is generally a solitary occupation, mine soon became a house of secrets.

If a love letter is the place where the innermost self is spoken, if letters to a loved one take the place of a private journal *(I must tell you everything – I no longer write in my journal; you are my journal . . .)*, then when the love letters stop, one's thoughts, if they cannot be spoken, build up into stores of words that must be housed elsewhere. Mine were enclosed in black and white note books in tiny scrawl, so small I can barely read it today. And there hidden they grew – like monsters of the deep.

I need to write to him and explain how when I speak to him lately, I go numb, and forget what I really need to say to him, which is essentially unsayable anyway . . . this need I don't know how to express just goes unsaid, unspoken . . .

Really, I was profoundly unhappy – as much as I loved Sydney and felt I should be expanding there, I was contracting. I spent much of my time at the kitchen table, reading Simone de Beauvoir, burning my fingers over the little bar heater in a cottage not made for winter, writing letters back to the States, writing in my journal, waiting to receive letters, waiting for Jonathan to come home from work, but feeling whatever it was that was 'us', disintegrating around me. *Before, writing to you was all I had of you. It was your hugs and kisses, your voice, your hard body, it was my dear desperate love, and now?*

We are not letter-lovers but real ones. But I still miss writing to you – waiting for a letter each day.

I no longer knew who I was. I was no longer American by location and I had not yet become Australian.

By June, I had come to the definitive conclusion that the only solution to the problem of how to be both a lover and a writer, how to both have *and* long for, how to be here and there, involved another geographical separation.

I went away so I could communicate, because I couldn't communicate otherwise.

At the end of a June day spent cycling alone in the Blue Mountains, I asked a shopkeeper in Wentworth Falls if they knew of any rooms to rent. An hour later I had found an empty, rather run-down gardeners cottage at the back of the old, run-down homestead on Falls Road. Pale white wooden walls, a brick fireplace, no hot water but lots of light, and a toilet with a door would eventually open onto a blossoming apple tree full of bees. The Christian family that was renting it out offered it to me for one dollar a day. I deemed it a perfect place to hunker down in my romantic illusions and write.

By the end of August, with three months left on my visa, I had moved to the Blue Mountains.

At the time, I thought this move absolutely necessary for my survival; later, I wondered if it had been unkind to Jonathan. Now that I know myself better, I see in this decision a refusal to dissolve in somebody else's arms. I had to move in order to find a place in Australia for me alone. It was a determined and full self that insisted on a change that would let me breathe again – breathe and bloom.

Even though it's only for three months, it is still three months out of my little life and I want it to be good. Inside, I know that if I can't be a writer in this way, in absolute solitude, then I don't have the tenacity to be a writer at all.

I enacted separations so that I could write.

Or, put another way: I enacted separations from love so that I could write love letters.

I realise that nurturing relationships with other people is healthy, however, I'm beginning to know that I'd rather spend that nurturing time writing letters to those people . . . There is almost nothing that I like better than writing letters and there is nobody that I know better through letters than you, my fingers know you best . . .

While the distance functioned ironically to lament distance and kept love alive (although a retreat from that very intimacy), it also became a real way of learning myself. I became a mountain of solitary, high above the entangled forest of daily love that threatened to engulf me.

So it was natural that the last thing I expected to happen up there was to fall in love.

It was a secret love, like a betrayal, but one that I could not shake. It was an impossible love because I could not stay there. But I was in love with the air, its wind-blown breathlessness, with the stark, orange cliffs, with the freedom of riding my bike to the edge of the world, with the ever-changing weather and sky, with bushwalking and standing with my neck bent back letting the waterfall mist land on my face and knowing, suddenly, with absolute clarity, that when I die I will soar here, over the Jamison Valley, like the wide-winged black cockatoos.

I was twenty-three and falling in love.

With Australia.

But like any new long distance love, it was written on the page from day one that we would have to part.

> I have your picture in my room. I never pass by it without stopping to look at it; and yet when you were present with me, I scare ever cast my eyes upon it . . .
>
> – Heloise to Abelard

I was lying on the floor of my apartment in Milwaukee; I was lying naked on the wooden floor of my apart-ment. My eyes floated open. A boy stood above me, fully clothed. He was looking at me, his hair flopped down over his eyes, his boots straddled my hips, the rubber soles of his Doc Martens pinched my skin, he leaned closer, a rock in his fist, he squatted down over me and placed this shard of sandstone on the dip of my stomach. It was cold. My belly contracted but I couldn't move. My arms were pinned to the floor by a row of gum leaves, my hips by his stance. The light fell in patches over me, snagged on the quartz, prismatic; my breasts fell full to the sides. I was becoming a map of Australia, my naked body soon covered with the rocks and shells and feathers and gumnuts of my new love.

He lifted a camera to his face. He was my lover, but I was in love with his country. My love for Jonathan was now absolutely twined with Australia, by which I meant the Blue Mountains, by which I meant the Jamison Valley, by which I meant Mount Solitary. It haunted me, my lost, longed-for misty mountain; that distant orange and blue cliff monument to my solitude. There it stood in all weather, strong, defiant, superior and separate. *Some days it was pink, and some days the shadows hugged the hills and deepened them until their greens stumbled . . . and some days the clouds hung so low, tired of moving . . . pulled thin and wet and draped over the jutting rocks . . . Such loneliness for my tiny green cottage. I cannot seem to get over it . . . or shake my longing for the mountains . . . What do I have now except the memories, its presence etched into me, the writing I did there and a few shoeboxes full of odd collected remnants which have lost some of their meaning in the transport? Broken clay roof tile with the mould of a bumblebee, a pile of sandstone rocks on my dresser with no sun to catch their sparkle, cracked macadamia nut shells, dried wattle flowers . . .*

He stayed with me in Milwaukee for three months,

then we returned to Australia. Remaining in America was never an option for us – I was fixated on coming back here.

Looking back now on the story that would carry me from one side of the world to the other, from being a girl named America to something altogether new, I am struck by how quickly and strongly I became connected to (more like obsessed with), the concept of Australia. Australia as a lover, almost, a long distance lover, a place, alive, breathing, somewhere on the other side of the world, without me, waiting for me I hoped, though I knew that ultimately, despite its heat, it was too cool to care whether I came back or not. Australia, my lover, had the power over me. I was just the girl worshipping at its feet, lapping up every grain of sand from its shore and sandstone core that came my way, laying out my transported treasures around me like an aura I hoped would attract its attention. I was a woman before a date, trying to turn my house into a place my lover would recognise himself within. I placed stones on window ledges, with both Jonathan and Australia firmly in mind, hoping to catch a shaft of a faraway light.

I made and loved and tended to this space around me – it was all I had. I hid here every day from Milwaukee – I hid here from this life I was forced to come back to . . . I made this space mine. I made it for me, for my independent self and I made it into Australia, to pretend I was still there and I made it into Jonathan, choosing things thinking of him. Then Jonathan arrives and he stands for Australia in a way that's more powerful than this place can ever stand for Australia, and so, it no longer can. 'I made this place into you and now you're here. It should disappear . . .' The photos of him scattered around fade, lost now, and my collections seem out of place as symbols of a land he now symbolises (not more strongly, not because he means Australia to me more than the rocks do, but I cannot deny the strength of his real presence).

I am struck by how the language of love infuses my letters and journals of the time; how romantic love gets transposed onto the idea of a continent, like lines hand-drawn onto the parchment that will eventually become a map.

I can't help but think about Australia . . . it invades me, like a virus, like a sweet smell and then it's inside me and it won't go away.

How transparent my letters of that time were – my romantic agenda for the lucky country and me. Sentences full of my genuine affection for Jonathan (for I did love him) finish with phrases destined only to touch the heart of my big wide land. *I can't imagine my life without you and I'm so scared right now, as you are, about what will happen, yet some days, most days, I feel I'll die unless I go back to Australia, that I can never really be happy outside it.* I now no longer wonder at his suspicion that I loved Australia more than I loved him; I just wonder that I couldn't see it better myself.

The truth is this: I could be with him anywhere. For me it is easier to stay in the States near my family and friends, because I do need them, more than he seems to need his (although maybe he is pretending). My love for him remains in either place. I am going back for the love of Australia . . .

How do such things get articulated? I wanted to be in Australia because of what Australia had come to mean about who *I* had become. This was a new self, a growing-up self, a writer in a cocoon; a self that was forming outside the boundaries, geographical and cultural, of my American childhood, and it developed a way of seeing the world that was not-American. Was it, was I, becoming Australian? Was I Australian if I loved Australia or just if I loved an Australian boy? Because Jonathan was not just my logistical link to the place, he was my heart link as well. I could not see the country without him standing in it.

Black cockatoos pair for life. You can walk along the creek at Wentworth Falls to the edge of the Jamison Valley to see what the clouds, the sea of fog and the blue air is doing to Mount Solitary. Two black cockatoos land on the heavy gum branch at the edge of the Falls, pick at each other for a moment, rub heads, and then, seemingly without warning, one bird is falling through the air, and the second bird is right behind it. It seems to me that they just threw themselves off the branch so effortlessly, without word or gesture, without complicated communications, one after another, two lovers; there was not a fraction of a second between the impulse of one and the leap of the other.

But who leads and who follows; which bird gets to choose the way to go?

Over the years the letters dwindled as lives fused, diverged. It was natural; people were busy. Then they dwindled more. There was a drought of letters, a shortage in the world market, yet unlike most shortages, the value of a letter didn't seem to exponentially rise in relation to the relative impossibility of finding yourself in possession of one. There was no black market for letters, no dirty trade on the back streets, no code word for the exchange of communiqué in glass beakers, or scrolled so tight upon themselves they could simulate cigarettes, tucked behind ears, dangling from twitching mouths, winked and nodded in dark corners of the world, traded like secrets, like the crystal speak of drugs. They remained alive only in places that still needed them, in prisons, detention centres, in love. In solitary confinement where a brave word from another, stealthily passed on toilet breaks, was enough to stay

alive just one more day. In exile. The world no longer had need of the letter proper and so, like organs disused, like fads long forgotten, like creatures that couldn't quite hack the modern world, those folded white sheets faded, until the words and the people they told, simply disappeared . . .

My most recent relationship has ended. We also lived at a distance, both geographical and emotional, the distance of two selves, each locked into our own worlds; two quartz crystals without the sediment to glue them together, to build rock. He did not write letters. I wrote few. For three years our relationship was conducted using the phone, mobile phone and landline, text messages and the occasional email.

My younger self might have been horrified by this loss of poetry, but perhaps this relationship was more haiku than epic, its corresponding trauma more samurai than troubadour.

But occasionally, whenever I felt the tug of the inex-pressible soul, I would write him a letter. Because while the instruments, the technology, of love have altered, there is still nothing like the carving of words into a page to tell another heart who you are; there is nothing like the secret an envelope holds; or the distance it has to travel before it will be unwrapped and savoured by the soul and eye a thousand times. Perhaps my younger self would be comforted to know that love grows again and again and that it grows somehow deeper, although

changed, with age. Each subsequent relationship – which
is, after all, really a relationship with yourself – grows as
you do. The distance you are bridging in love is a distance
with the self. I wrote to others so that I could understand
love in myself; so that I could learn who I was; so that
I could set it all out on the page like an equation and try
and find a solution to the hurt of my own distance.

The road I've carved winds from Milwaukee,
Wisconsin (how random those two words seem now, as
if childhood origin was merely a spot on the globe from
which I would arrive *here*) to Sydney, from Sydney up
to the Blue Mountains. It is, more than anything, a road
to writing, a story of becoming a writer; a road that was
carved from blocks of love. I think it has a happy ending.

Once upon all those years ago, after a long day's
bushwalk to Mount Solitary, I wrote:

*Some day I will look back, half-remember the colour
of the light on the path and the special, private ecstasy
of solitude and accomplishment I am feeling. The light
moves from the sky through the blue oil and when it
arrives on the path in front of me, it is a rainbow that is
only one colour. It is the colour of a feeling that even now
seems indescribable. Some day I will wonder, 'It's true?
These moments are mine?'*

In an Old Frame

KENDALL HILL

In an old book – about a hundred years old –
  forgotten among its pages,
I found a water color unsigned.
It must have been the work of a very able artist.
It has as its title, 'A Presentation of Love'.
But more fittingly would have been, 'Of Utter Sensual
  Love'.
For it was evident when you looked at the work
(the artist's idea was easily understood)
that the young man in the painting was not destined
to be one of those who loves more or less healthily,
remaining within the limits of the more or less
permissible – with chestnut, deep-colored eyes;
with the exquisite beauty of his face,

the beauty of deviate attractions;
with his ideal lips that offer
sensual delight to a beloved body;
with his ideal limbs created for beds which
current morality brands as shameless.

– Constantine P Cavafy, 'In An Old Book'

Cam recognised a fellow traveller when he saw one. He once told me that reading Cavafy was like reading his own thoughts on a page. The gay Greek's poems reassured him that no matter how unconventionally his life unfolded, someone else out there – someone halfway respectable – had been there before and knew exactly what he was going through. I trawled through more than a hundred of Cavafy's works before I found this one. It seemed the most appropriate to Cam.

So I have this poem to prompt me into the story. (It's been a while since I last told it.) And I have an old framed photo. The image has dulled a little with time, the silvery gloss of the Aegean now more of a slaty glimmer. But the light is still warm and rich, and Cam still looks every bit the shining youth full of promise and hope.

The picture hangs in my study, above my desk. Cam is seated, knees drawn up towards his chest and held there by folded arms. His deep tan is offset by a white singlet and trousers. He seems to be gazing out to sea; the faded water stretches behind him until it reaches a peaked mountain, an ancient volcano. His long lashes are shielding the sun, and at the corners of his eyes is a reminder of that familiar squint, his trademark. He used to crinkle the corners of his eyes as if straining to make sense of the world around him.

In the top right of the photo there is a large metal cylinder, like a silo, with two solar panels on its roof. It's hard to tell exactly what it is, but I suspect it's part of a ferry and Cam is on his way back to Paros, another Greek summer unfolding languidly before him. That would explain the carefree smile.

I have many other photos from Paros, all taken after that one, but they don't tell the whole truth. Holiday snaps only ever capture the happy moments. There is no record of tears or anger or jealousy. They're not the things we want to remember.

These other photos live mainly in loose packets in old shoe boxes; a few favourites have made it into an album. They show the joy of reunited friends; sun-drenched lazy meals at quaint waterside *tavernas*; a beautifully hack-neyed scene of blue shuttered windows and tin-can pots of geraniums against a whitewashed wall; lunch at a hilltop café in the quaint town of Lefkes, where butter-flies skimmed the air and nuggetty old men played the local version of bowls on a village green beneath bald-ing pines. A field of wildflowers with a blue-domed monastery at its centre. Sunbathing on Lagiri beach, the daily ritual. Philippe in the garden of his home, hugging young Jamal to his side. With their smooth features and dark skin they look like father and son.

But there are no more photos of Cam. He was already dead by the time we got to Paros.

Our stories all have identical beginnings and conclusions – only the bits in the middle are interesting. This story begins with an ending, but it will show how an ending can become a beginning, and how death is not always the end.

Very late one October night Cam was killed riding his motorbike near his home on the Greek island of Paros. The story I heard was that he and his French lover, Philippe, had one of their regular blues that night and Cam stormed out. From hearsay – half-truths and suspicions cobbled together after the event – it seems he rode his motorbike into town, spent the next few hours drinking away his anger at one of the port-side bars, then made the fatally stupid decision to hop on his bike and ride home.

As he neared the hilltop house he and Philippe shared, Cam overshot their dirt-track driveway. He must have tried to wrench his bike into a U-turn, at speed, which caused it to fly out beneath him. He managed to keep his grip and flew with the bike until man and machine hit the ground. His head smashed onto one of the low, dry-stone walls that trace the island, and he died instantly. He was twenty-nine.

When the news filtered back to Australia a few days later I had no idea what to feel. I joined his other closest friends, in bars and each other's homes, where we recalled him as best we could through a veil of alcohol and cigarette smoke. Grief was such a foreign emotion that I spent most of those miserable hours wondering if I was saying and doing the right things. My uncertainty wasn't helped by the fact that in recent years I hadn't seen Cam for more than a few weeks in total.

Aside from its tragic ending, Cam's Greek life was largely a mystery to me. Occasional reports from friends who'd been to visit him kept me up to date with the highlights – how he'd started out selling sandwiches on the beach from the back of a donkey, how he'd met Philippe, how he eventually landed a waiting job at the coolest restaurant in Naoussa, Paros's idyllic fishing port.

Now I was being forced to remember Cam, I realised how little I knew of his later years. Just the edited highlights and the closing credits.

Will, Cam's closest friend, organised the memorial service at a crematorium in Melbourne's outer northern suburbs. The setting was suitably cheerless, beside the Hume Highway in the drought-stricken grounds of a blandly functional chapel. Within the dull brick walls Cam's life was recalled by a large photo-board on the altar, the tear-choked eulogies of his friends and a selection of his favourite music.

The wake was back at the rambling terrace house where Cam had lived with Will for years before he went away. I relaxed in the familiar surroundings and, for the first time in days, felt free to be myself again, reassured by the knowledge my friend had been given a sincere send-off. Cam's mother came back to the house too, and wedged her small body into a safe corner of the upstairs lounge where she sat blinking and bewildered in the midst of her son's drunken, teary friends. Most of us were strangers to her but we crowded around as she told us stories of a boy we never knew, and we told her stories of a young man she didn't recognise.

A few weeks after the service, Will made copies of that photo of Cam and distributed them among his friends as a final keepsake. The photo and our memories were all we had left of him then, and they didn't seem enough. It felt like we, eight of his closest friends, should at least go to Paros and say a proper goodbye. Love and the bonds of friendship dictated that. And returning to Cam's adopted home would give us the chance to understand a little more about him, we figured. Help us fill in the gaps of his life since he'd quit Melbourne for a little fishing village on the other side of the world.

It is more garden than cemetery – a garden with head-stones instead of statuary, where visitors have birdsong, cool shade and memories to keep them company.

Almost every tomb is covered by a bed of potted flowers, each chosen to best reflect the tastes of the inhab-itants beneath. There are pots of geraniums, rampant roses, simple daisies, rosemary for remembrance, pansies, nasturtiums and, on one grave only, a thriving grevillea bush amid the usual floral line-up. This is Cam's place.

The grevillea is sturdy and brilliant, its leaves that shade of smoky green that defines the Australian bush. It is smothered in vibrantly exotic, honey-orange firebrands of flowers. Philippe said the local birds were wary of the grevillea at first but, over time, they grew to like the little stranger. If you hang around Cam's grave long enough you'll notice the locals have become fond of the Australian plant too. They all drop by to admire it, but most of them know by now not to lavish it with water or to nurture it in any way. It's a fiercely independent plant, feisty and determined. Much like Cam.

'*Philos*?' asked the woman, smiling as she stopped by Cam's grave on her way back from the tap with a full watering tin.

'*Okhi*,' I said. No. She asked something else but with my limited grasp of Greek I wasn't up to understanding her. I smiled awkwardly, embarrassed by what I couldn't say to her. She smiled too, an uncertain flash, then bowed her head and left to resume tending a grave. I realised later I should have said *nai*, yes. I thought *philos* meant brother but it means friend.

Early mornings were loveliest at the graveyard. The sun was high enough, and the sky blue enough, to guarantee another flawless day. On the way from my seafront apartment, the streets were usually empty, their cobbles silent except for my footsteps. Docile cats would slowly warm themselves into the day on sunny slabs of white-washed stone.

There was an easy camaraderie between morning visitors at the graveyard. We greeted each other with a cheery '*Kalimera*' at the tap while waiting to fill our watering cans. I'd make a few comments about the weather – enough to exhaust my Greek – then head back to Cam's grave to water the plants, tend them, and light the oil candle. It sat inside a glass lantern on top of the tombstone among the pot plants. As I lit it I'd look at Cam's crinkled face in the photo behind and have a little conversation with it. Usually in my head, but it didn't matter; the voluble Greeks often spoke to their dead out loud.

Most evenings, at sunset, a parade of *yayas* – Greek grandmothers – would arrive, their candles lighting the dark and reflecting off the Parian marble of the graves. Cam's headstone had been carved from this famed local stone so it was a favourite landmark for the women.

My friends and I all paid regular visits to his grave that summer. It felt like an unspoken duty, the logical consequence of having come so far to see him. I went alone most times.

I can't picture what Cam looks like in that graveside photo any more. It was only a tiny image, barely bigger than a passport photo, and once the oil candle was lit his features were thrown into shadow. I could make out his eyes, serenely brown, but the rest I filled in from memory. Just as I'm doing now.

I also made a pilgrimage – twice – to the spot on the road where he died. I felt uneasy riding my rented motorbike down the hill from the village, turning right onto a barren track and retracing the route of his misfortune.

Just past Cam and Philippe's old house on the hill was a white column with a glass case at the top. Inside was yet another photo of Cam and another simple oil lamp, to be lit by passing well-wishers. When summer finally cooled and we'd all gone back home, it was up to Philippe to keep the fire burning. Cam's constant companion, even in death.

I'm not sure who found him first that night, or who raised the alarm, but Philippe said the reaction in Naoussa had been immediate and extraordinary. When the villagers learned of his death the order went out for the church bells to be rung, a rare honour for an outsider.

The version of events I'd been told in Melbourne was so patchy, and there were so many gaps in my understanding of Cam's last years, that I'd left Australia brimming with questions for his European friends. Had he been happy? How had he spent his days and months and years here? Did he ever mention me? But here on Paros the questions sounded insensitive and wrong, so they went unasked and unanswered.

Philippe isn't the most talkative of men anyway. He is, by and large, as arrogant as the French archetype though he can be outrageously funny, warm and sincere.

He just chooses not to air his better qualities in public very often.

I knew him a little from a trip he'd made to Melbourne with Cam. It was an arduous week during which Philippe complained constantly and I, for one, couldn't wait to escort him back to Tullamarine and see him through the departure gates. I tried to like him, for Cam's sake, and I put on a good show of hospitality and kindness, to little effect. Philippe would accept dinner invitations then sit sullenly at the table, acting as if he'd been forced to endure the company of imbecile cousins. He paid scant attention to anything any of us had to say. To a man who'd quit Paris for the pleasures of life on a Greek island, I realised I must have seemed pathetically provincial. But that was no reason to be rude.

When I met him again in Naoussa he was that familiar impossible prince, but over the course of the month we managed to fashion something approaching friendship. Philippe proved he was capable of great compassion and thoughtfulness, though his usual state was one of benign insolence. As far as he was concerned, whatever had brought me to his island was my business. If I had come to piece together Cam's life, I'd have to do it on my own.

Philippe made his feelings clear the one time I raised the issue with him. I was at his house late one night early in the holiday. We had been drinking, which made things easier, and I just came out with it: 'So, can we talk about Cam? I feel like I know nothing of his life here.'

Philippe frowned, annoyed, then brooded in silence. He probably could have remained that way indefinitely, but patience has its limits.

'Philippe. Are we going to talk or not?'

He raised his head slowly. 'I am not very good at compromising,' he said.

'What's compromise got to do with it?'

'To share my memories with you would compromise them. And compromise me. My life . . . so much of my life is shaped by Cameron, even now. And I know that if I discuss those moments with you they will become less real for me. If I have to share them then, of course, I will be left with less.'

I must have been drunk because his argument made perfect sense. I was certainly in no state to argue that sharing did not leave you with less. So I let him lapse back into silence and never quizzed him about Cam again.

What I do know. Cam was born at Williamstown Hospital in April 1966. His father, Jim, was a boilermaker at a chemicals plant out west; his mother, June, was a domestic help for the plant's general manager. In his late thirties, Jim was diagnosed with the first of the malignant growths that would eventually kill him. By the time he was forty-two, his body riddled with deadly mutations, his son and daughter knew him as little more than a bedridden invalid addled by morphine. He wasn't a figure who inspired much emotion in his children, although some days as they fidgeted by his bed, surrounded by medicines and the familiar trappings of their father's illness, they could stare into his eyes and see something approaching love shining out. Then again, perhaps they were confusing love with the warm glow of morphine. They were too young then to make such distinctions.

Jim died at forty-three, when Cameron was in grade five. He was not a brilliant student but what little promise he had shown dwindled with the death of his father. His mother spiralled into despair and was in no state to help him. Cam said her resentment and anger had been festering for years, ever since his father took permanently to bed, but his death was the trigger that unleashed all that poisonous misery. She raged against the world, against her lot, and against her son.

Cam had always had a keen instinct for survival (except on that last night) and at fifteen he fled the family weatherboard and moved in with Will. The pair had met just months earlier in the midst of Melbourne's nightclub scene, and they bonded instantly.

I met Cam a couple of years later. He was one of the many characters I bumped into at the bar or on the dance floor, but he had a charisma and a charm that drew me to him. He also had insight and wisdom, and was a terrific anchor for anyone like me, drifting uncertainly through a belated adolescence. But his most valuable trait was that he knew how to party.

There was no one like Cam to drag me out and show me how to enjoy the illicit pleasures of early adulthood. He had a tremendous appetite for debauchery after dark, but it was tempered by a sober daytime routine of waiting tables, gardening and cooking.

At his and Will's house there were no set rules, so it became a haven where we experimented with everything and everyone, making mistakes on the way to adulthood safe in the knowledge that we would not be judged or mocked or reprimanded. It was an invaluable freedom as we tried to work out who we were and what we were capable of.

Cam wasn't tall, about five eight, and he dressed invariably in faded jeans and white T-shirts smelling of Cold Power. He wore heavy boots that gave him a bit of height, and his only concession to Melbourne's long bitter winters was a tatty denim jacket. He was a dark-haired James Dean, in the right light. And he was always shivering.

Other things I remember about Cam: Sade (the singer, not the sadist), barracking (usually unsuccessfully) for the Demons, photography, prowling on the dance floor, his crinkly laughing eyes, his unassuming confidence, the warmth of his friendship. Cam was tough, reckless, head-strong, endearing, and hilarious. He was the entertainer, the rebel, the eccentric, the darling. But they're only words now, not fully formed ideas of who he is. All I recall are snatches of talent and temerity that barely convey how central he was to my young life.

More than ten years since his death, my memories of
Cam have dimmed like his photo, leaving just an outline
that lacks the fine detail I once knew by heart.

It was no great surprise when he announced he wasn't
coming back from Europe. Anyone could recognise a
chance like that – a stab at a new life beyond his imagin-
ings. Only a real escape, one that put thousands of miles
between him and his past, would give him the freedom to
start fresh.

On his last visit to Melbourne, after he'd been in Greece
for two or three summers, Cam had clearly changed. There
was not really one identifiable thing about him that was
different – it was more that I made the realisation,
common enough in your twenties when you're making
long-term decisions about friendships and love, that our
bonds had loosened a bit. We used to have something solid
and tangible; now it was nice but uneasy.

We still regarded each other as close friends and had
the reassurance of all our shared memories, but nothing
came as effortlessly as before. When we met it felt as if
there was more silence than talk, as we struggled over the
awkward gaps in our mutual knowledge. Relaxed
laughter gave way to almost apologetic smiles. Remin-
iscing about old times stirred glimmers of the ease and
warmth we once knew, but nostalgia can only tide you
over so far before it starts to feel as if you're avoiding the
present. So we'd switch back to the present, and soon
come up against another episode that wasn't shared;
something new and awkward standing between us.

Throughout his stay in Melbourne, whenever we met we continued to pretend it was just like catching up with an old friend, but it didn't feel that way. It was uncomfortable. Our lives had diverged and we didn't have common reference points any more. I was provincial; he was European. It seemed to me he had higher expectations of life, and I no longer met those expectations.

His changed manner – and mine, I guess – reminded me of a conversation we'd had when he was about to set off for Greece the first time. We were having farewell drinks in a Spanish bar in Fitzroy and I quizzed him about what his plans were.

'What do you think you want to do with your life?' I asked, as much for my sake as for his. We were both at a crossroads of sorts.

'I don't have any firm ideas,' he said. 'I just know I want to be surprised by life. I want to wake up every day and look forward to what's ahead, but I don't mind if I don't have any real idea what it will be.'

I told him that sounded more like a mission statement than a plan. He laughed.

'That's exactly what it is. I don't want to set goals or have anyone else set them for me. I'm going away to escape all that. I want to live somewhere anonymous where no one has any preconceived ideas about who I am or how I should act.

'And I can't do that here. There hasn't been any comfort for me in Melbourne for years. Why else do you reckon we're having a drinking session at midday on a Friday?' Cam had a gift for putting our lives into perspective.

As soon as he'd saved enough money to buy his next ticket to Greece, he left. I don't think he had any intention of coming home for good again. The news he sent back from Paros was short and very sweet: he'd met Philippe, he would stay on the island working over summer then would divide his time between Athens and Paris in the winter. What a life, I thought.

I guess I went to Paros that summer, at least in part, in the hope of rekindling the bond we once had.

One of Philippe's friends had come to Naoussa at the same time we were there. Khalida was a dark Algerian beauty, very gamine, who lived in one of Paris's grim outer suburbs. She shared a small apartment with her son, Jamal, whom she brought with her. She was in her early thirties and Jamal was seven.

They were cool, those two; I always felt loud and gauche around them. Khalida often joined me and my friends but Jamal rarely ventured out with us as a group; he preferred to stay with his Uncle Philippe at home, where he didn't have to grapple with our unfamiliar faces or our very poor French. On the few occasions when we were all together the Australians competed for Jamal's attentions – he was stuck-up but easily bought – and courted Khalida. All we wanted was some acceptance.

Khalida's indifference to me melted away during a day trip to the dreamy Cycladic island of Amorgos. The ferry dropped us at the pretty port of Katapola, with its pastel-washed buildings reflected in the glassy sea. From there a bus drove steeply up to the main village of Hora, population 500 or so. It was lunchtime, and we wandered into the first place with octopus on the menu. The combination of the comforting food, a few drinks, the setting and her growing familiarity with us softened Khalida's mood. She laughed at our jokes and offered snippets of her life in Paris driving taxis by day and caring for Jamal at night, alone. She'd loved his father, she said, but knew she could never tie him down. Her pregnancy had been an accident but not a completely unhappy one, so she set about preparing herself and her home for motherhood.

'Do you see the father any more?' I asked.

'Not for some years, no.'

'Do you miss him?'

She sat there toying with an unlit cigarette and concentrating that disarming gaze of hers on me.

'You don't stop loving someone just because they're gone from your life,' she said. 'I think you know that. He is always a part of who I am, and even more so a part of who Jamal is.'

Jamal, who was on a rare outing with us, didn't acknowledge his name when she said it. But I was used to his temperament by then. There was no real language barrier between us; he spoke enough English to make himself understood but he usually kept his own counsel. He preferred conversations with his mother or Philippe, and always in French. On the odd occasion when he did hazard a question to one of us – when those two were busy or absent – he would ask them the same question later as if he didn't trust what we'd told him. Maybe he just didn't understand our accents.

After lunch we began the long slog to the Byzantine monastery of Panagia Hozoviotissa. This was a type of pilgrimage, too, like going to Cam's grave or visiting the roadside memorial where he died. He used to love this island, especially the gravity-defying monastery at the top of the hill. He knew the myth of the monastery by heart. A statue of the *Panagia*, or Virgin Mary, was said to have washed ashore here after a shipwreck in the ninth century. A passing fisherman discovered it and heard a voice telling him to build a monastery at the island's summit to house the icon. So he did. Cam got the whole improbable story from one of the priests there, when he and Philippe visited one spring. Cam came back a couple of times and fell more deeply for the place. He was always at Philippe about moving to Amorgos. Which is why Philippe hadn't joined us that day. He said he couldn't go back without Cam.

The stunning structure is now a drawcard for the island, and the few tourists who make the detour to Amorgos hike up there to pay a visit.

We trudged along a desolate road cut into a scree-covered hill. Rocky cliffs dropped down into a sea so intensely coloured it inspired a movie, *The Big Blue*. The famous lagoon of Agia Anna shimmered mirage-like and we wished we were there rather than on this desolate hillside. The clouds were heavy, the air thick and steamy and our clothes were glued to our bodies with sweat. It was hard at that moment to imagine why Cam had treasured the place so much. Only the surreal sight of the white-washed, geo-metric tumble of the monastery spurred us on.

At the entrance a monk looked disappointedly at our skimpy clothes and told us we would have to don robes for modesty. We wore cover-all, smocky kaftans that somehow managed to look quite flattering on the girls but laughable on me. We scaled the claustrophobic sauna of a stairwell and emerged onto the upper terrace, where the privations of the journey suddenly seemed worth it. Euphoria, one of many useful Greek words, perfectly describes how we felt on first catching that superlative view across the Aegean. You're perched on a terrace at the top of a mountain, surveying a chain of Greek islands. Views don't come much better.

As we stared out at the brilliant blue, Khalida caught my eye and gave me a tiny half-smile. I smiled back and she moved closer, slipped her arms under mine and hugged me from behind. It was a rare display of affection for her.

'*Quel est beau!*' she sighed. How beautiful!

'The sea?'

'Yes, of course, but I meant the world. All of it. I'm always surprised at how pretty it is. Even in the most horrible places, you can discover the beauty if you try.'

I laughed. Not because what she'd said was absurd, but because it seemed obvious she would say that. So long as she had a mirror nearby, Khalida's world would never be without beauty. Her tanned Berber complexion, twinkling black-marble eyes, coarse cropped hair and crooked, heart-shaped face weren't conventionally pretty but – at moments like these, when she was happy and laughing – they were irresistible.

Back at the port, while the rest were busy with ice-cream, Khalida and I wandered along the shore past fishing boats painted in lurid colours, sporting eyes to ward off bad luck. We stopped under a pine for a smoke.

'You know,' she said, taking a drag as I sat down beside her, 'Cameron was not like you.'

'What do you mean? He was one of my closest friends.'

'Of course you were friends. But you were not very similar.'

'Why do you say that?'

'When Cam came to Europe, he settled in very quickly. It was like he'd found home. He appreciated the *esprit*, the openness of our societies. Even here in Greece, where everyone is so pious and superstitious at the same time, the people let you live as you wish.'

'But what does that have to do with Cam?'

'Cam was not someone who liked being restrained.'

'Everyone knows that.'

'Yes, but I think he had a difficult childhood, and as an adult he did not have much direction. So here he became a hedonist; no rules, only fun.'

I smiled at her, recognising my friend and guessing he'd found his dream life, full of surprises.

'What did he enjoy doing most?'

'Oh, everything. He loved men, naturally, and culture and music, and he had an appetite for drugs – though he was not what you would call an addict. He just enjoyed the release, like the rest of us. And when he was high, that's when he most loved to go exploring in Paris.'

'I can imagine,' I said, but really I couldn't. When I tried to visualise what he might have got up to my mind drew a blank. I closed my eyes and tried to imagine his Paris nights but all I saw was black. The same shade of black that obscures so many of my memories of him now.

'Did he ever get into trouble?'

'You know Cameron,' she smiled. 'If he had a problem he was so discreet that no-one would find out. And if they did, his friends were very loyal. They would never discuss those things.'

'If he had been in trouble, would you tell me?'

She didn't answer. Just flicked me a look.

'Look, you know I came here to find out more about the years I missed of Cam's life, and to say goodbye to him. And ever since I arrived it's like you and Philippe have made a pact not to talk about him. Philippe barely mentions him; you haven't told me anything about your time with him. You won't tell me what Cam did here, how he lived. And I can't tell you how frustrating that is.'

'I'm sorry,' Khalida said, smiling again but with a firmness that closed the topic. She took her cigarette butt

from the dirt and rose to her feet. Conversation closed. We
headed back to the ferry in silence, her only consolation
being to grab my hand just before we reached the boat. It
was something.

Khalida seemed to relent after our port-side chat and
talked to me about Cam more often.

She told me how he went to Paris that first winter,
newly attached to Philippe and brimming with the excitement of it all. Cam and Khalida first met then, and by her
account it was not a wildly happy time for any of them.

Will had been to visit Cam in Paris and reported back
that Philippe and Khalida carried on like a newlywed
couple – always touching each other and flirting –
whenever Cam wasn't around. All three had felt threatened by each other at first and it showed in the
awkwardness of their company. 'Philippe was not the
same with me, nor I with him, and neither of us knew
how we should be around Cameron,' Khalida confessed.

The wary trio used alcohol and hash and whatever
else was available to dissolve the barriers between them,
with encouraging results. Cam regained some of the
passion he'd had with Philippe in Greece, and managed
to fashion a mutual respect with Khalida.

When they weren't workshopping their relationships,
Cam loved to lose himself in the wintry city. There was a
cemetery in Montmartre he would visit often. He loved

the grace and opulence of the elaborate tombs, always topped by sculptural flourishes such as weeping angels or Madonnas.

There was a little street he loved too, at the base of the Sacré Coeur. It was cobbled and charming – he once showed me a photo of it – and he would spend hours there lingering over an omelette and a glass of cheap wine, watching the city scurry past and keeping an eye out for the unusual and amusing.

Khalida was a wonderful storyteller, able to conjure the atmosphere and mood of Cam's days in Paris, but I guessed there was plenty she wasn't telling me. She suggested as much when she said: 'I wish you could have known Cameron here in Europe because then you would know the person I knew. It's strange for me when you talk of this other "Cam", because the more you describe him in Melbourne the less he resembles the man I knew in Paris.'

She was right. I only had to cast my mind back to his visit to Melbourne to recognise how changed he was. And being on Paros was proving to be a constant reminder of how dramatically our lives had diverged.

Far from re-establishing a connection with him there, I only felt further removed. It was like I'd finally caught up to where he was, but he'd already moved on, and there was no way now to contact him again. Some days, drained by the futility of the experience, I would contemplate going home early. There didn't seem any point staying on. Cam certainly wouldn't miss me.

But something always happened that convinced me to stay. Or, more correctly, Khalida always sensed my mood and took it upon herself to lift it by sharing confidences and making me feel valued. That's how I found out that Philippe didn't despise me after all.

'I know you think he hates people, that he is rude, but I think it is more a case of hating himself a little, too,' Khalida confided towards the end of the holiday. 'He is not the easiest person to be friends with but once you get under that rage he is really wonderful. And he likes you – you must know that. He is very touched that you have come this far to pay tribute to Cameron.'

'Did he say that to you?'

'You know Philippe. Not in so many words. But I can tell from the way he acts with you – the way he teaches you Greek words because he knows you are interested, and the way he always asks after you when we've been out for the day. Not to your face of course, but he asks me. And he is not the sort of person to throw anyone a birthday party unless he really wanted to. Do you remember how lovely it was that night?'

Of course I did. It had only been a week since my party. It was at Philippe's new house, on the other side of the island to the one he'd shared with Cam, on an isolated hill with only stars and the sea below for neighbours. Khalida had smuggled half a dozen mini champagne bottles from her Air France flight and had them chilling in the fridge for my arrival. There were nine of us there, both locals and foreigners, but the others kindly left the champagne to me.

Around 10 pm, when a breeze finally arrived to cool down the night, we saw red lights bobbing in the sea below, heading for port. It was beautiful to watch. Philippe explained it was the annual re-enactment of the invasion of Naoussa by a Turkish pirate called Barbarossa. The Turk lost, repelled by the villagers, and annual fireworks displays now re-enact the battle and celebrate Naoussa's victory. The partying typically goes all night.

It was a memorable evening. Philippe had been charming but distant, as ever. I'd given up worrying about his moods after Khalida told me that if I really wanted to understand Cam I had to try harder to understand Philippe.

'He is the one person Cameron chose to spend his life with,' she said. 'And you know he had terrific taste. When you speak negatively of Philippe you ignore his capacity for love. It is very great. He just doesn't reveal it willingly.'

'No. He never has to me.'

'I doubt he will. He doesn't think you are a very passionate person. Funny, yes, and intelligent, but not a man of passion. He doesn't think you would understand.'

'Understand what?'

'That love can be volatile. That there doesn't have to be controls. That you can choose to ignore them.'

'What sort of controls?'

'You know these already, I'm sure. Social controls. Controls that say you should live your life a certain way.

Based on religion, or superstition, or silly beliefs that have stood unchallenged for centuries. We know some boundaries are there for a very good reason, but others exist simply to save people from being scared. They exist in the name of order, and order can be so boring.'

'But I know that already.'

'Of course you do. But what he is suggesting, I think, is that you are perhaps more bound by those controls than we are. We all know they are there, but those who choose to ignore them or disobey them tend to keep their actions to themselves.'

'I don't get your point.'

'All I'm saying is that everyone has secrets, and regrets, and private triumphs and tragedies they will never share openly because they don't feel they can. When you ask me what Cameron's life was like here and in Paris, I only give you the answers I am happy to reveal, and that I think you will accept. And anyway, I don't think you would believe my stories even if I told you.'

As it happened, Khalida didn't need to say a word about her best-kept secret. It revealed itself.

It was her and Jamal's last day. For a treat he'd decided to come swimming with Khalida and I and three of my friends from Australia. It was the first time we'd seen Jamal in a week or more. They weren't leaving for Athens until late afternoon so we met at eight at Kalypso café for our usual breakfast of honey, yoghurt, fruit and Greek coffee. Afterwards we strolled along the pier and made the 9 am ferry. At that hour it was just us and a couple of fit-looking Germans heading to Lagiri beach, our usual haunt.

The hours at the beach passed the same as all the others. We mapped out our spot of pebbly shore with towels, books, Walkmans, lotions. We smothered ourselves in oil, then drifted in and out of consciousness all day, catching snatches of conversations when we came to. And there was plenty of swimming, of course. For lunch we bought sandwiches from a boatman plying the waters.

It was a relief to leave early and escape the thickening crowds. We had the three o'clock ferry largely to ourselves. The sun was low on the water, turning the ripples into flashes of silver. Jamal was beside his mother, staring west into the sun at an island in the distance. Naxos or something.

His long lashes were drawn low to filter the sun and the corners of his eyes had crinkled a little. Into a squint, as if he were straining to make something out, the way Cam used to do. Exactly the way Cam used to do.

I kept staring at Jamal, waiting for this mirage of a resemblance to vanish. But it didn't. Caught in this light, and with this expression, Jamal looked just like Cam. Just like his father.

I turned to Khalida. She was staring back at me and I could tell by the flash in her eyes that she knew I'd worked it out. She began shaking her head very slowly, careful not to attract anyone's attention but mine, almost willing me to disbelieve what I'd seen. When she summoned enough courage to mouth a defiant 'No!' at me, I could tell she only did it out of desperation. Then her eyes started pleading. I looked back at Jamal, at the evidence, and felt . . . I don't know what. Numb is too mild a word. So is stunned. Absolutely winded and bewildered and shocked comes closer to describing it.

Khalida looked away, out over the top of Jamal's head. The breeze whisked away the forming tears. Her eyes dropped to study the sunlit profile of Jamal's face, and with a glance back at me she seemed to concede it was useless pretending. The truth was obvious; the only mystery was why it had taken me so long to see it.

When our boat docked at Naoussa Philippe was there with his car and their bags, as arranged, ready to join us for a farewell drink before driving them to meet the ferry at Parikia. But there was no farewell drink. He knew from our faces that the game was up and bundled Khalida and Jamal straight off the boat and into his car. We didn't have a chance to say goodbye before they sped off.

Philippe claimed to be too busy to see me in the days that followed. In an uncommon burst of generosity he'd promised to drive me to the ferry on my last day, but instead sent a message that he was sorry he couldn't make it – work commitments. He hoped I had a safe flight home to Australia.

Before I arrived in Paros it had seemed implausible that Cam would ever father a child. But having seen the proof, in Jamal, it didn't seem quite so far-fetched a concept any more. Totally unexpected, yes, but plausible now.

I haven't seen Khalida or Jamal since that day. I don't know whether Jamal has ever been told who his father is. He must be around eighteen now, old enough to know the truth.

Sometimes I wish I'd made a scene on the ferry that afternoon and forced Khalida to explain everything. But with Jamal there, and not knowing how much he knew or how much it would hurt him to find out in front of everyone, it was impossible.

I don't think about that Greek holiday much any more. There's little point reliving it because I always come up against the same unanswered questions, and I've exhausted my theories on all of them. I know as much as I'm ever going to know about Cam's life. And about Jamal's. But I'm glad I got the chance to say goodbye.

Ten years on, Cam is more than just a photo. He's two photos. The one of him on the ferry, and another that hangs beside it of a seven-year-old on the same sea, in the same light, the same expression on his face. The same face even, just a few shades darker. When I look at them both together on the wall, they remind me that there's no point digging for more answers, that this is all I need to know.

In Praise of Coffee

VALERIE BARNES

We met in Geneva in the early 1970s during an inter-national telecommunications conference. He was the leader of the Australian delegation chairing the meeting from behind a microphone on the podium, one hand pressing an earphone closer for fear of missing a word. I was the interpreter high up under the ceiling in one of the glass interpreters' booths facing the podium, leaning forward as I concentrated on each speaker. Between us sat 2,500 delegates from the 127 member-countries of the United Nations, in neat rows at tables with microphones at regular intervals. They had their backs to me and each also sported an earphone.

His voice had a buttery warmth that appealed to me,

so all through that long meeting, I made my voice sound as sexy as possible. In my line of work, voices are very important: I need to comprehend immediately what's being said so I appreciate qualities like clarity and calmness. From so high up I sometimes cannot see faces down below very clearly, so voices might be all I have to go on.

Although I enjoy interpreting, I was thankful when the chairman announced a break and I could race off for a quick cup of coffee. Like most simultaneous interpreters I am addicted to coffee. Just as cars need petrol, we need coffee to keep going, to keep our brains fresh and alert and ready to tackle the unexpected. Still to this day, if I haven't had my mid-morning coffee, I start to fade and shrivel and turn into a prune.

One morning during just such a much-needed coffee break, a delegate came across to tell me that he had seen someone rather like me onstage in a Gilbert and Sullivan production the previous evening. I recognised his quiet buttery voice as that of the committee chairman for whom I had been trying to sound sexy, so I didn't mind at all that he broke in on my morning coffee. He introduced himself as Peter.

I was struck by the intense blue of his eyes and their mischievous sparkle, his boyish look and his handsome tan. It was only when reflecting on our conversation later that I realised that he had just come from an Australian summer to winter in Geneva.

'She was very much like you to look at. Taller and

slimmer perhaps but there was a definite resemblance,'
he continued.

Amused, I let him waffle on for a bit before finally
cutting in to say: 'Actually, it *was* me. I was in *Ruddigore*
last night.'

At his confused look, I explained that I was a member
of the UN Gilbert and Sullivan society. He was embarrassed, which I found rather endearing. We chatted on
over our coffee. I told him how I loved singing and especially becoming a carefree 17-year-old maiden twice a
week – though sometimes I would have preferred to be
Katisha in *The Mikado* so I could rant and rave instead
of always being sweet and demure. I didn't mention how
lonely my life had become since my divorce or that I
enjoyed rehearsals as much for the company as the music.
We talked until the meeting reconvened and I had to
hurry back to my high perch, more determined than ever
to make my voice sound as captivating as possible.

In the conference cafeteria later that week, Peter asked
if he could join me at lunch – I was sitting alone at a big
table. Some of his colleagues joined us and soon I was
surrounded by Australians all asking questions about
simultaneous interpretation. Glancing out of the window
I noticed black clouds gathering, so the moment I finished
eating I jumped up and, apologising, explained that it
looked like rain and I was going to dash home to bring
in the washing.

'Let me come and help,' offered one of the Australians
(not Peter), so we rushed out of the building, leapt into

my turquoise Fiat 127, and shot off along the autoroute in a mad dash to get to my village seven kilometres away before the rain came down. We made it, and got back to the conference before the afternoon meeting started at two o'clock.

That was the start of our little Australian group. I sensed how much they missed family life. Most of the telecommunication conferences in those days lasted six weeks and after a week or two of hotel life even the simplest domestic chore, like bringing in the washing, was a welcome reminder of home.

Most delegations gave a reception during the first week or two of a conference to help everyone get to know one another and when it was the Australians' turn they asked me for a list of the interpreters' names, so they could be sent invitations. In those days, there were very few women conference delegates and the Australians complained that all-male cocktail parties were getting rather boring.

The Australian party was held at the Vieux Bois, a restaurant on the hill behind the Palais des Nations, the European headquarters of the UN. As leader of the delegation Peter greeted all the guests on arrival but seemed to pay me particular attention, finding me a glass of wine and introducing me to everyone, and I thought he seemed considerate, polite and charming.

During the evening, Peter confided that he had a lot of difficulty getting the point of what one of the delegates was saying.

'I sit there with my pen poised, intent upon taking notes for my report, but there seems to be nothing I can pin down, no bottom line; just words. Do you understand what he's getting at?' he asked. 'There seems to be no thread through what he says.'

I had interpreted for this particular delegate many times before. 'He says everything three times,' I explained. 'By the third time his thoughts are clearer and he has a better idea of what he wants to say. Just concentrate on that third time.'

Later he said: 'If I invited you out to lunch, would you accept?'

'I might,' I replied as I walked away, smiling.

After that, each morning when I rushed to consult the noticeboard in the interpreters' room to see what my assignments were for the day I started to secretly hope that the chairman of my meetings would be Peter of the buttery Australian voice that made maritime distress signals sound almost interesting. Sometimes I was lucky.

The six-week conference was drawing to a close. We worked long hours during the last week – there were night meetings until the early hours as the delegates realised how far behind schedule they were and as the deadline for signing the Final Acts fast approached. We were all overworked, tired and irritable but when the texts were finally approved by the Editorial Committee and just needed to be printed for the signing ceremony on the last day, everyone relaxed. On the evening before the ceremony I was invited by the Australian delegation to the Longchamp Hotel where they were all staying. The occasion was a bottle-emptying party: everyone brought the last of their duty-free supplies to be finished. I wore my favourite dress but the evening was a disappointment – Peter wasn't there. He had been called away to a policy meeting with the president of the conference.

The Final Acts were signed around midnight on the last day by the leaders of all the delegations. It was then that it suddenly struck us all, tired though we were, that this was the end. All the hard work was over. The bonds of friendship that had been created were about to be severed. Removing my headphones, I threw all my now-obsolete documents in the wastepaper basket and picked up my handbag ready to leave. I wanted a chance to bid Peter farewell before he left the building. But looking down into the hall, I saw the delegates milling about saying goodbye, exchanging business cards, some shaking hands and others kissing one another on both cheeks and suddenly felt that it was not my place to go into the meeting room to say goodbye to anybody.

As I was leaving the building, I heard footsteps behind me.

'How about that lunch we talked about?' a welcome buttery voice said. 'Tomorrow? I don't leave until late afternoon. Say, Perle du Lac at 12.30?'

'Perle du Lac it is,' I replied, and headed off towards the carpark feeling elated.

It was a beautiful day. The sky was the particular deep azure you see only in Switzerland. After lunch we walked along the *quai* looking at the yachts. The lake was bluer than I had ever seen it and dotted with sailing boats. A weekend regatta was probably in progress.

'My plane goes soon – I have to go back to the Longchamp to pack,' Peter said finally.

He accompanied me to my car. We turned to each other to say goodbye and suddenly his face seemed to come into focus, every detail as clear as an etching. His eyes were the same intense blue as the lake. I could see the sailing boats on the lake reflected in them. I held out my hand to shake his and thank him for lunch, but suddenly both his strong hands were on my shoulders and he kissed me full on the lips. Then he turned and walked away.

Stunned, I got into my car and sat quietly for a few minutes to regain my composure. It was a long time since I had been kissed on the lips. In Geneva, you kissed people on the cheek, even husbands and wives. Kissing on the lips was something very personal that rarely happened outside the bedroom or at least in the dark. I didn't know how to interpret what had just happened.

I'd never met an Australian before: perhaps it was an Australian custom for men to kiss women on the lips at the drop of a hat? Maybe all Australian men kissed women on the lips if they had taken them out to lunch, or did Australians kiss everyone on the lips all the time? I was shocked, yet I was intrigued and couldn't stop thinking about what had just happened. Indeed, for the next few weeks as I sat in the booth in yet another conference, talking about single and double side band, side lobes and tropospheric scatter, all the time my mind was playing with the thought of that kiss . . .

Some months later a maritime radio conference opened at the Conference Centre. I hardly dared hope Peter would be there but, looking down from my glass interpretation booth, I saw that he was.

We started spending all our breaks together, taking our cups of coffee off to a secluded area behind the coffee bar so we could talk without interruption. One evening after work we drove into nearby France and had dinner in a homely little restaurant with red and white check tablecloths and matching curtains. We decided to go for a walk afterwards but I was wearing smart high-heeled shoes, and when we started off down a steep grassy slope towards the lake, my feet carried me away until I was running faster and faster. Fortunately Peter managed to catch up with me and hold on to my arm to slow me down. It was only the second time he had touched me and we were both a little embarrassed.

When he told me how boring his weekends were, mostly working and meeting up with the rest of his delegation in the evenings at the only English-speaking pub in Geneva, the Pickwick, I offered to take him sightseeing. We decided to go away the following weekend and every coffee break that week was spent poring over maps spread out on the table. In the end we went to Le Pont, on the Lac de Joux about fifty kilometres from Geneva. It was an exciting moment when we set off, our overnight bags in the boot of my trusty Fiat. It was getting dark when we arrived, having lost our way several times. Peter went to enquire at the only hotel while I waited in the car, wondering whether he would book separate rooms – I had felt too shy to ask. The hotel's restaurant was closed but we were able to get a ham sandwich and a glass of wine. Then came the moment of truth: it was indeed one room.

The following morning we sat at the end of the bed having breakfast from the hotel tray. Peter cut the rolls in half and buttered them which I found quaint but charming. I had never seen anyone cut bread rolls in half with a knife before. In Switzerland, we always broke them into pieces and ate them like that. The crusty French bread rolls tasted good the way Peter prepared them and to me it was a novelty.

We climbed a mountain and, at the top, lay in the grass and talked. Beneath us the countryside was lost in mist. We knew so little about one another, there was a lot to tell and I was curious to hear what Australia was like.

We had fondue for lunch. I explained the rituals and we laughed each time Peter's piece of bread came off his fork and he had to pay a forfeit. It seemed that all the people around were smiling at us because we looked so happy.

After three wonderful weekends together I was afraid my joy would show on my face and our colleagues would guess what had happened between us.

On the fourth weekend we went camping.

Peter had been very keen on the idea, but I couldn't see the point of sleeping on the ground in a tent when there were plenty of comfortable hotels with soft beds and hot showers. However it seemed important to him and he explained it was very Australian to go camping so I finally agreed to try.

Fortunately for me the whole thing was such a fiasco that I never had to go camping again. It rained both days. Bravely we tried to fry sausages over a campfire in the drizzle but our raincoats and the umbrellas got in the way. Night fell very quickly and we had to put up our tent by torchlight. Our sleeping bags were damp to start with, then in the early hours I discovered that mine was sopping wet and so was I. Peter had gone out of the tent in the night and forgotten to zip up the flap properly when he came back because it was dark and he was half-asleep. All in all, as disasters go, it was pretty successful.

As we sat in the car, sheltering from the rain, he told me he had been separated from his wife for some two years and had been living with a younger woman he had met at work. But the new relationship wasn't working either and they were both unhappy. He had been spending sleepless nights trying to find a solution that wouldn't cause too much pain.

One evening a lavish cocktail party was to be held by the American delegation. We had both received invitations but decided not to go: we would have a party of our own in Peter's hotel room instead. There would be little chance of me being seen on my way there because everyone would be at the US reception. It was very romantic: in his tiny kitchenette, Peter had managed to prepare a three-course dinner. There were candles on the table, red roses in a vase and even a gift on my plate – a hand-embroidered handkerchief, neatly wrapped in shiny paper with a little note. As I took it all in, something clicked and I understood in a rush that what had seemed a brief affair was taking on quite a different aspect. Despite our best intentions, we were falling in love.

But in an attempt to be sensible, we decided to keep things light – after all, we both enjoyed our independence and had lives of our own. So when inevitably the time came for Peter to go home to Australia, I drove him to the airport but didn't get out of the car.

'No promises,' he said.

'No promises,' I agreed.

A quick kiss and his smiling tanned face disappeared behind the glass doors. And I drove back into my other world.

For many months after that, we communicated by aerogram. Do they even exist any more? They were sheets of flimsy paper that folded and sealed to form their own pale blue envelopes. We each sent at least one a day, sometimes two – on occasion I received three, carefully numbered. They were covered with writing, with extra bits written up the sides, in the corners and even in the space meant for the return address. There were always PSs, sometimes even on the front around the address. Peter's spidery handwriting was quite a challenge under these conditions. We told each other everything that had happened that day and how much we missed one another. He wrote that he had finally broken off his unhappy relationship and was now staying with a relative. Sometimes instead of aerograms I received fat envelopes with hotel addresses from Singapore, Bangkok or Jakarta – wherever his work took him.

But we did manage to meet occasionally, when our work

brought us to the same city or we were able to snatch a few days together. Our time together may have been brief but it was always very intense and long afterwards we remembered every detail. Sometimes we behaved like crazy teenagers, tightrope-walking along narrow walls with outstretched arms or giggling helplessly as we walked backwards along the street, just for fun. I remember Peter jumping up into a tree to frighten me as passers-by glared at us disapprovingly. On a beach somewhere in England we were eating icecream cones as we strolled along the sand when he drew a magic circle around me with his foot so that I was protected from harm forever. The row of old people sitting in deckchairs above the beach watched incredulously to see what we would do next.

One birthday, Peter gave me an invisible box and when I opened it, he told me to be sure to look at the picture inside the lid.

'What is the picture of?' I asked.

'Whatever you wish,' he replied. 'It changes all the time. It is magic. You can choose your own picture.'

On one particular weekend together in London a very important event took place: Peter liberated me from my corsets. He was amazed that I should wear such a garment. It seemed that Australian women were far more emancipated. One day when we were having lunch at

Swan and Edgars on Piccadilly Circus, he assured me that I would look perfectly normal without corsets and that it was not necessary to be uncomfortable in order to look right. So I did something I thought very daring: I went to the ladies' room, removed my corsets and put them in the rubbish bin. I never wore any again. Instantly I felt carefree and, when I think about it today, I still feel a bit of a daredevil.

Almost a year after we first met I travelled to Australia for the first time. Peter was waiting at the airport with a bunch of carnations. He took me to a serviced apartment he had rented for us in East Melbourne where there were more flowers, a fridge full of food, a cassette player and a pile of tapes, bars of chocolate, bottles of wine and other treats. Then he hurried off to work. Every morning he told me where to meet him for lunch in town. In the meantime I explored Melbourne, especially loving the wonderful parks filled with trees and flowers unlike any I had seen before. I also saw my first black swans and still wonder why they are white in one hemisphere and black in the other. (Do they have swans anywhere along the equator and are they half white and half black or simply grey?)

On our first evening he took me to a French restaurant for dinner. The menu was full of spelling mistakes but I thought it tactful to say nothing. Melbourne was very crowded because of the annual Moomba festival and I spent a lot of time looking around the various festival events, especially the art and sculpture exhibitions. Sometimes I wandered with Peter along the Yarra River, watching the college teams rowing. We spent our weekends on the beaches, which were so much more beautiful and less crowded than the ones I was used to.

As an interpreter, I have always been fascinated by local sayings and have made quite a collection over the years. So I was delighted to learn a few Australian expressions like 'to go crook' and 'he feels crook' but 'she'll be apples'. And to discover that when people referred to a hotel they generally meant a pub, that a chicken was a chook and I was a Sheila, and that some people were 'whingers' or 'dole bludgers'. I also heard classics like 'to come the raw prawn', 'fair dinkum', 'true blue', and 'it's your shout' for the first time.

For my last weekend we visited Pambula Beach in NSW, ten hours' drive from Melbourne, where Peter's parents lived. They gave me a warm, open-armed welcome. There were paintings everywhere because both were artists. I remember a mauve tablecloth and a bowl of blue and pink asters in the centre of the table, and white roses on my dressing table. We visited the local beaches and strange rock formations and that night we slept in the same bed Peter had slept in first with his wife and then with his next partner.

As we sat eating our breakfast on the balcony outside our room, two butterflies played love-games, fluttering and chasing one another among the flowers. Strange that, all these years later, we still remember them.

Then back to Melbourne and the usual quick airport goodbyes: brave face, stiff upper lip, no lingering. And we were back to aerograms. But now, we found, they no longer satisfied. Being apart was a bit like having a toothache that only went away when we were reunited.

We planned our first holiday together: two glorious weeks on a Greek island, but at the last minute Peter sent a telegram to say he could get away for only five days. By the time we got there we were both exhausted from work and travel. He had spent more than twenty hours in the plane and had only one desire: to sleep. I tried all the tricks I could think of to keep him awake, but he would nod off at the most inconvenient times. We did have a few beautiful moments: leisurely evenings in a nearby café drinking ouzo or retsina at square wooden tables while the boats alongside tipped lazily this way and that; a boat trip to nearby Lalaria to see a famous rock with a big hole in it and admire the marble-white beach and powder-blue water. But by the time Peter had recovered from jet lag, our time together was coloured by his imminent departure and everything we did and said was bathed in pathos. Peter said he would telephone me for my birthday, a few days later, so as I settled in my seat in the plane home I realised I had that to look forward to at least.

When I got home to Geneva and found all the flowers still fresh in their vases, I could hardly believe I had been gone at all. Yet at the same time those five days had been so intense they almost felt like a lifetime.

Some five months later we attended the same conference in Kyoto, Japan; something we had been looking forward to for ages. The conference building was magnificent, looking out onto a boating lake with shiny gold and red fish darting about in the water. It was surrounded by weeping willows and a park where Japanese couples met to walk decorously in the shade of the trees. The girls wore or carried wide-brimmed hats and were dressed in full skirts and lacy tops; they gave the impression of being coquettish and very shy.

The opening ceremony for the conference was held in the afternoon and was followed by a magnificent reception. I wore a long Empire-line brown georgette dress and Erika, my interpreter colleague and booth-mate, said I looked like Marie-Antoinette. I was pleased, until she added: 'Or else you must be pregnant'. All round the hall were stands offering different types of food, including my favourite – tempura. On the stage, music played and dancers performed amazing acrobatic feats with sticks and yoyos, bells and drums. Every type of drink you could think of was available. The women were dressed in silks, furs and jewellery and the men smelt of expensive aftershave. Walking round the room greeting all the people I knew, so many different French perfumes wafted my way that I felt quite light-headed. Later the most spectacular firework display I had ever seen took place outside over the lake. Peter and I sat close together on the steps of the building, our knees touching, his arm round my shoulders. We ooh-d and aah-d with everyone else at each new dazzling explosion in the sky. The finale was the title of the conference lit up in fireworks that sparkled and exploded in all directions.

As our first weekend approached, we decided to go on an adventure. I wanted to stay in a *ryokan*, a Japanese-style hotel. I had done that on previous trips to Japan and had found that living the Japanese way felt like being in a different world. So we decided we would take the *Shinkansen* – the new bullet train – to a little country village for the weekend. We didn't book anywhere, we thought that we'd just jump off if a village took our fancy.

The weather was very hot and in preparation for our weekend trip I bought myself an elegant white *broderie anglaise* parasol with a frill round the edge. (Sunhats just seem to make my head hotter.) I loved my elegant parasol and it matched the white cotton dress I planned to wear.

Saturday morning we were up early and off to the train station. We queued at the ticket counter but when our turn came we didn't know the names of the train stops or where we wanted to get off so we couldn't say where we wanted to go. Somehow we got tickets to *some-where*.

The beautiful, modern, streamlined bullet train was absolutely silent yet extremely fast. It ran so smoothly not a drop spilt from our brimful coffee cups even though the speedometer on the buffet car wall read 200 km/h. Through the windows we glimpsed a series of traditional scenes: stills of rice farmers in broad-brimmed straw hats, ancient-looking villages and tall-legged birds wading in ponds.

When the train stopped at the pretty town of Kurashiki with its canal bordered by weeping willows we agreed this was the place and jumped out. Walking hand in hand through the little town we saw no other non-Japanese faces and were constantly stopped by passers-by who asked if they could take our photograph, or who wanted to try out their English on us. The most common thing we were asked, especially by groups of schoolchildren, was 'What is your name?' but when we told them they just giggled.

We spent the night in a *ryokan* as we'd hoped, sleeping on *tatami* – rice-straw mats just two centimetres thick – on the wooden floor. My dressing table was so low I could only see into the mirror by sitting on the floor. The half-sized box of tissues produced half-sized tissues. First we had a very hot Japanese bath, waiting timidly until everyone else had left. Then, dressed in the kimonos provided, we ate a dinner served at a low table in our room. I found I slept surprisingly comfortably on the *tatami* with a wooden neck rest. And if you slept on your back, your hairstyle was intact the next morning. In fact, if you happened to wear a complicated interwoven Japanese chignon, you probably only had to have your hair done once a week at the most . . .

I loved the Japanese way of leaving your street shoes outside and relaxing in comfortable house-slippers. Also, you didn't have to approach the toilet door at the end of the corridor with stealth, trying the handle as quietly as possible to see if someone was inside, because from afar you could see the pair of slippers outside, their owner having hygienically switched to the toilet slippers inside. I was particularly fascinated by the little jump combined with a twisting hip movement I had never been able to catch anyone doing to get your feet out of your corridor slippers, leaving them facing in the opposite direction, ready for when you came out. Everyone seemed to be an expert at it except me.

I was sorry to leave beautiful Kurashiki and the *ryokan*, but Peter was quite happy to get back to a proper bed.

Most evenings there was a conference cocktail party hosted by one or other delegation; sometimes we went out on the town afterwards to the 'MayBe Pub' or a nightclub. The cabaret shows were very innocent: girls traditionally dressed in white kimonos danced and sang, accompanying themselves on a sort of Japanese guitar.

They also, apparently, told jokes. But we weren't paying attention – we were in a world of our own. Often when we got back to the hotel we were so happy we did high-kicks all the way along the long corridor between our rooms, giggling like children and hoping that none of the conference delegates in the rooms we passed would hear us and recognise our voices.

Another time we had dinner in a smart waterside restaurant, seated on cushions at low tables. The reflections of dozens of paper lanterns all round us shimmered in the water. A Japanese hostess in a beautifully embroidered kimono squatted between us at our table cooking the *sukiyaki* and refilling our *sake* glasses until, having had too much and overcome by the romance of the occasion, Peter bent and kissed my toes that were sticking out from beneath the table, just next to him. This rather shocked the Japanese diners around us and we suddenly felt it was time to leave.

One evening the Australian delegation was invited by the president of a Japanese company to a cocktail party in their high-rise offices. I too was invited – I seemed to have become an honorary Australian. All the men were sampling Japanese beer. Now I have never been able to drink beer for pleasure ever since I breastfed my three children in Switzerland and the Swiss–German nurse insisted I drink a litre of beer every day to ensure my milk supply. So when the president honoured me, one of the few women present, by asking me what I would like to drink, I asked for a gin and tonic. At this request, the eyes of the inexperienced young waiter taking the order seemed to fill with panic. At length he reappeared with a tray of bottles and a large glass which he then proceeded to fill almost to the brim with gin, topping it off with just the smallest splash of tonic water.

Aghast, I stared at it then desperately looked around the room for Peter to come and rescue me. At last I spotted him laughing and chatting with a group of Australians over a glass of beer and completely oblivious to my plight. Surely, I thought, after we had been so close he must be receptive to my ESP messages. But apparently not. Everyone was being so polite and there was so much bowing I despaired of ever attracting his attention. I knew what I had to do: I had to drink what was in my glass so the company president wouldn't lose face – and for the honour of Australia.

I took a tiny sip, then another.

As I continued distractedly chatting to the company president and taking sips of nearly neat gin, someone took our photograph. Happily I have never seen that picture, but the flash of the camera drew Peter's attention at last. I was beginning to perspire and the room was spinning round me. Daintily I continued sipping until I started swaying on my feet and mercifully Peter finally hurried over and took my arm.

'I'm not feeling well, please take me back to the hotel,' I managed to gasp. Peter grabbed my elbow firmly and after a few polite words to the president we headed for the revolving glass doors that led out of the offices and Peter pushed me forward into one of the compartments.

I was safely in – but the problem now was how to get out. I tried to lurch in the right direction each time I reached the exit but by the time I had organised myself to take action, the moment had passed and I was revolving helplessly again. This went on for quite a while, until Peter, by now outside, managed to grab me and drag me out. Then there was an escalator and a lift to negotiate, a taxi, then another lift at our hotel and finally the long corridor lined with the rooms of the conference staff and delegates that I had to be dragged along while Peter did his best to muffle my giggles. When finally I lay on my bed, he mopped my forehead with a cool wet towel, frantically trying to stop me singing (which I was very keen to do, apparently) because he knew that if anyone recognised my voice, my reputation and my future interpreting career might be in jeopardy. To his great relief I suddenly fell asleep and he was able to creep out and return to his own room.

My most cherished memory of the Kyoto conference is of our lunches. On the top floor of the conference building was a staff cafeteria where everyone went – everyone, that is, except for Peter and me. We had a much better plan and every detail of those lunchtimes stays in my mind like a living photograph.

Towards the end of the morning, I would slip out of my booth and take the lift up to the cafeteria to buy supplies for a picnic. The food was rather a mystery but the uncertainty added an element of adventure to the day. I once chose a selection of pretty little parcels wrapped up in brightly coloured paper, twisted at each end like chocolates or toffees. I thought we would enjoy them for dessert but they turned out to be Bombay Duck.

With my dainty Japanese carrier-bag of food and drink secured, the moment the chairman announced 'The meeting will now adjourn until two o'clock' I would hurry out of the booth and down the stairs to where Peter was waiting by the boatshed outside the building. We'd jump into a hired rowing boat and he'd row us off. The man in the boatshed began to recognise us after the first few days and would give us a knowing smile as he prepared our boat and passed me my parasol once I was installed on the seat.

The lake was still and green with the reflections of the trees. Occasionally there would be a ripple as a fish came to the surface, snatched a passing insect and disappeared again in the depths. We tried different weeping willows until we found the one we liked best and after that we made a beeline for it every lunchtime. There in the seclusion of the willow branches we were in our own private world. We would unpack our picnic. Very little was said – there was no need for words. The gently rippling water and the quiet, with only the occasional passing family of ducks to disturb us, created a world of serenity around us. After lunch it was siesta time in the bottom of the boat – but it had to be a one-eye-on-the-time siesta for I had to be back in the booth by five minutes to two.

This time it was even harder to say goodbye at the end of the conference. We both knew by now that this was more than just a fling. After these interludes, the transition to my other world was always jarring – I was never quite prepared for it or its finality. But this time my Geneva home had never seemed so bleak, nor Australia so far away.

Peter wrote or telephoned every day. Sometimes there would be a gap and then I would receive a bundle of five or six aerograms all at once. We continued to spend many hours writing to tell one another every detail of our daily lives.

Until a time came when there was nothing: no letters; no telephone calls. I felt as if I had been cut in half. Whatever could have happened? I got more desperate each empty day, imagining calamity. Perhaps a car accident. A heart attack. Or some kind of natural disaster – surely only something very terrible could prevent him from getting in touch? I searched in vain for an Australian newspaper or a mention of Australia, but the only reference I could find was in the *New York Herald Tribune* which reported a mouse plague down under. It was difficult to see how mice could prevent a telecommunications expert from communicating with Geneva. It wasn't until several weeks later that I learnt he had been travelling all over Australia with a team of satellite experts. They were installing a state-of-the-art satellite communications system involving geostationary orbits. All that communications expertise and no way of contacting me!

Ten frantic days went by. I kept posting aerograms but received nothing in return. And then one night I was awoken by the strident shrill of the telephone. The voice I longed to hear said: 'It's me. I'm in Canberra.'

Fighting back the sudden onrush of tears so they wouldn't spoil this precious moment, I gulped and said: 'Thank heavens you've phoned – I've been so worried! I've been calling and calling you. We need to talk: I think I'm pregnant. What are we going to do?'

I heard Peter mutter something unintelligible at the other end. Perhaps there was something wrong with the line and he hadn't heard me. I repeated what I had said a bit louder, and added plaintively: 'I've been feeling very sick and my period is late.'

Then I was interrupted by a strange, authoritative male voice: 'This is a demonstration call over the new satellite communication system,' it intoned, to my horror. 'We have asked our international expert if he would like to inaugurate the system and he has chosen to call a number in Switzerland. This conversation is being broadcast worldwide by satellite . . .'

As it happened, it was a false alarm: I wasn't pregnant after all.

We were in love but to me, marriage was out of the question. After my long, unhappy marriage ended, I had promised myself – and my friends – never to re-marry. A life of freedom and fun was what I wanted with no commitments, no problems. I would take lovers of course, choosing them carefully so there would be no complications. I would be spoilt and pampered, showered with expensive presents and travel the world on luxury yachts to exotic destinations. I had tried marriage and once was enough.

And then one Saturday morning the telephone rang six times.

As I mentioned earlier, I need my morning coffee to function properly, and woe betide anyone who comes between me and it.

The first time the telephone rang just as the kettle began to boil. I guessed the call was from Australia and therefore expensive, so reluctantly I switched off the kettle and answered the telephone. We talked for twenty minutes or so and the last thing Peter said was: 'Will you marry me?'

'I'll need time to think about it,' I replied rather tersely. What I meant was 'I need my cup of coffee first and *then* I'll think about it'.

I switched the kettle on again, the water boiled and just as I was about to pour it into the filter the phone rang again. This happened four more times . . .

The smell of ground coffee was getting to me. In fact, I have always thought that the smell of freshly ground coffee beans is even better than the taste of the coffee itself. I would have said 'yes' to almost anything by the time the phone rang for the sixth time.

About the Authors

EMILY BALLOU

Poet, screenwriter and novelist Emily Ballou was born in Milwaukee in 1968 and in 1991 moved to Australia, where she completed a Masters in Gender and Cultural Studies at Sydney University. In 1996, she was a recipient of the Australian Film Commission's New Screenwriters Scheme for her first feature film script, *Sadie X-Ray*. In 1997 she was awarded the Judith Wright Prize for Poetry for her poem 'Enter'. She has worked with Gillian Armstrong adapting Helen Hodgman's *Waiting for Matindi* for the screen and in 2003 wrote the screenplay for the Fox Searchlight funded short *Mittens*, directed by Emma Freeman. *Mittens* was Fox Searchlight's short film nominee for the 2004 Academy Awards. Emily's first novel *Father Lands* was published by Picador in 2002. She was chosen as one of *The Sydney Morning Herald*'s Best Young Novelists of 2003. She is currently writing a second novel, *Aphelion*.

VALERIE BARNES
Valerie Barnes has lived most of her life in Switzerland, but has worked for the United Nations all over the world. She speaks several languages, was kidnapped in Cairo, and was proposed to in an African country by the President, who wanted her for his fourteenth wife. Tired of airports, luxury hotels, lavish cocktail parties, official dinners and suitcases, she married an Australian in 1981. Her first academic book, *Conference Interpretation*, was published in 2000. Her memoir, *A Foreign Affair*, was published by Random House in 2004.

JOHN BIRMINGHAM
John Birmingham is the author of eight books and is a regular contributor to a wide range of newspapers and magazines. He has written cult comedy (*He Died With a Felafel in His Hand*), award-winning history (*Leviathan*), and big dumb airport novels (*Weapons of Choice*). For the next little while you'll find him living with his family on top of a high hill in Brisbane. He maintains a blog at http://birmo.journalspace.com.

SARAH DARMODY

Sarah Darmody is the author of *Ticket to Ride: Lost and Found in America*. Her previous jobs have ranged from the heights of global film production to the depths of Middle Eastern toilet cleaning and the big-grin thrill of working full-time with firefighters. Raised in Sydney but at home in the world, she now lives in Melbourne, where her cravings for long stories, good coffee, the affections of stray cats and the Boy can all be satisfied.

TOM GLEESON

Tom Gleeson is half of the *Tom & Subby Show* on Triple M and has performed his one-man shows at festivals including the Melbourne Comedy Festival, the Montreal Just for Laughs Comedy Festival and the Edinburgh Fringe Festival. Tom was a cast member on one of Channel Ten's highest rating programs, the sketch comedy show 'skitHOUSE', as well as appearing on numerous other TV shows including 'Rove Live', 'Good Morning Australia', 'Glasshouse', 'Stand Up', 'Sunrise', 'World Comedy Tour' and 'Good News Week'.

NICHOLAS HOPE

Born in 1958, Nicholas Hope emigrated with his family to Whyalla, South Australia, in 1966. He began his working life in the Savings Bank of South Australia, left to study social work, got mugged and became a clerk in the Staff Pay section of Australia Post. In 1985, he decided to become an actor. His first book, *Brushing the Tip of Fame*, was published by Bantam in 2004. He divides his time chasing work between Sydney and Europe.

KENDALL HILL

Kendall Hill is a journalist based in Sydney. He is a former travel editor of the *Sydney Morning Herald*, and he contributes regular travel stories to publications in Australia and the US. His story is a fictionalised memoir based on real events and people.

SARAH MACDONALD

Sarah Macdonald is a radio broadcaster, television presenter, journalist and commentator, best known for her work at the ABC's Triple J radio station where she hosted the Morning Show, Arts Program and covered political events in Canberra. Sarah also appeared on 'Recovery', 'Race Around the World' and 'Two Shot' on ABC Television. She wrote *Holy Cow! An Indian Adventure* in 2002 and edited *Come Away with Me* in 2004. Sarah now works as a casual presenter at ABC Radio's 702 and Radio National.

MANDY SAYER

Mandy Sayer is the author seven books, the most recent of which are *Fifteen Kinds of Desire* (stories), and the memoirs *Velocity* and *Dreamtime Alice*, which won the the 2000 National Biography Award, the New England Booksellers Award in the US, and has since been translated into several European languages. She lives in Sydney.

COME AWAY WITH ME
Edited by Sarah Macdonald

Led by the bestselling author of *Holy Cow!*, come away with some of Australia's most intrepid adventurers on a first-class trip around the world.

Share the joys of travel, along with a good beating in a Russian bathhouse with Irris Makler; French Disneyland à la Nikki Gemmell; love and longing in Portugal with Christopher Kremmer; loathing and paranoia in Nick Earls' London; an unlikely bikie culture in Peter Moore's Vietnam; the perils of Sri Lankan dinner parties with Tim Elliott; New York underground with Caroline Overington; a Chinese haunting with Annette Shun Wah; getting off the beaten track in Japan with Tony Davis; and discovering a whole other country after India with Sarah Macdonald.

HOLY COW!

Sarah Macdonald

'Well, madam, I will tell you one thing. You are back in India for a good shaking. Here you will dance with death and be reborn. You will be a chameleon of karma...'

After backpacking her way around India, Sarah Macdonald decides she hates the country with a passion. When a beggar at the airport reads her palm and insists she will one day return – and for love – she screams 'Never!' and gives the country, and him, the finger.

But eleven years later the prophecy comes true. When the love of her life is posted to India, she quits her dream job as a national radio presenter and follows him to the most polluted city on earth, New Delhi. It seems like the ultimate sacrifice for love and it almost kills her – literally.

After being cursed by a naked sadhu smeared in human ashes, Sarah almost dies from double pneumonia, but not before facing some serious questions about her fragile mortality and inner spiritual void – not to mention some unsightly hair loss.

It's enough to send a rapidly balding atheist on a wild rollercoaster ride through India in search of the meaning of life and death. With the help of the Dalai Lama, a goddess of healing hugs and a couple of Bollywood stars – among many, many others – Sarah discovers a hell of a lot more.

TICKET TO RIDE

Sarah Darmody

After a lifetime of winning nothing but the right to be designated driver, Sarah Darmody strikes it rich in a contest so bizarre most people think it's an urban legend – the Green Card lottery. Her prize: the right to live and work in America forever, all for less than the price of an instant scratchie. But it's going to cost her much more.

Fingerprinted, stripped, x-rayed, measured and investigated, she's warned that unless she commits serious time to her new country and uses her Green Card, she loses it. So, armed with an ugly red backpack, a tattered map, and a wad of hard-earned tips stuffed into her bra, she sets off to circumnavigate the continental US of A by way of another legendary American ticket to ride, the Greyhound bus.

However romantic it might look in *Breakfast at Tiffany's* Sarah soon discovers the Greyhound is more *Midnight Cowboy* territory, favoured by the desperately poor, the despicably odoured and the dubiously paroled. But as she gradually becomes at one with her fellow travellers on their private 'Jerry Springer Show' on wheels and is expelled into ever more amazing and improbable places, she begins to fall in love with her big, crazy, beautiful mixed-up new land.

Funny, fascinating, fly on the wall and literally edge of your seat, *Ticket to Ride* goes where no tourist has ever gone before .

LEVIATHAN

John Birmingham

'To peer deeply into this ghost city, the one lying beneath the surface, is to understand that Sydney has a soul and that it is a very dark place indeed.'

Beneath the shining harbour, amid the towers of global greed and deep inside the bad-drugs madness of the suburban wastelands, lies Sydney's shadow history. Terrifying tsunamis, corpse-robbing morgue staff, killer cops, neo-Nazis, power junkies and bumbling SWOS teams electrify this epic tale of a city with a cold vacuum for a moral core.

Birmingham drills beneath the cover story of a successful multicultural metropolis and melts the boundaries between past and present to reveal a ghost city beneath the surface of concrete and glass. In Birmingham's alternative history of Sydney, the yawning chasm between the megarich and the lumpen masses is as evident in the insane wealth of the new elites as it was in the head-spinning rapacity of the NSW Rum Corps. This is a city shattered by the nexus between government, big money and the underworld, where the glittering prizes go to the strong, not the just.

Combining intensive research with the pace of a techo-thriller, John Birmingham creates a rich portrait of a city too dazzled by its own gorgeous reflection to care much for what lies at its dark, corrupted heart. Illuminated by wild flashes of black humour, violent, ghoulish and utterly compelling, *Leviathan* is history for the Tarantino generation.

BRUSHING THE TIP OF FAME

Nicholas Hope

In the fly-on-the-wall tradition of David Niven's bestselling *The Moon's a Balloon* comes a hilarious take on what making movies and working with big – and small – stars today is really like . . .

As Andy Warhol said, everyone has a shot at 15 minutes of fame, but he didn't mention where. Being famous in Latvia or Lightning Ridge is a whole other animal to being famous in Hollywood. And sometimes being almost famous can be a helluva lot more fun. In the same year Toni Collette won an AFI Best Actress award for *Muriel's Wedding*, Nicholas Hope won Best Actor for a very different film, *Bad Boy Bubby*. The latter evaded blockbuster status and became a cult hit. So did its star. While Toni was jetting off to Hollywood to co-star with Bruce Willis in *The Sixth Sense*, Hope was heading off to Berlevåg to make a film about corruption in the Norwegian cod fishing industry.

But it's not all snow, home-burnt alcohol and quilted jump-suits. Being almost famous takes the boy from Whyalla all over the world, from the glamour of the Venice Film Festival as Best Actor nominee to a whole other sort of festival in Riga, from obscurity in New York to star status in Lightning Ridge. Along the way, he falls madly in love and meets more crazy people, famous and otherwise, than any former bank clerk from the bush could ever have daydreamed about. With a wonderful sense of the ridiculous, Nicholas Hope offers a thoroughly entertaining insider's view of a world he clearly loves despite all its flaws, and is never better than when he is laughing at himself.

VELOCITY

Mandy Sayer

A heartbreaking memoir of growing up from the acclaimed author of *Dreamtime Alice*.

Velocity tells the moving, painful but often hilarious story of Mandy Sayer's childhood and adolescence, a life lived on the edges – of society, of poverty, of certainty, of love. Filled with beautifully realised descriptions of life seen through a child's eyes – a child who gradually comes to realise her adored parents are all too tragically flawed and broken – *Velocity* packs the emotional impact of *Angela's Ashes* with the surreal humour and razor-sharp observations of *Running With Scissors*. Against a vivid backdrop of smoky jazz bars, steamy beer gardens and a succession of lino-floored dosshouses, Sayer brings into focus those moments when the child's world and the adult world intersect, when illusions are shattered and understanding begins. Unflinchingly honest, startlingly brave and written with a clear-eyed, lyrical grace, *Velocity* is an ultimately uplifting story of struggle and faith against terrifying odds.

A FOREIGN AFFAIR

Valerie Barnes

'Walking along the drab, grey streets past bomb craters and piles of rubble, I day-dreamed about a more romantic world where people spoke exotic languages, played music, and sang and danced with passion.'

Trapped in the austerity of post-war London, 20-year-old Valerie Barnes yearned for the good times promised by the wartime songs. Then two chance meetings catapulted her into a high-flying career at the newly formed United Nations in Geneva and the arms of a glamorous Frenchman . . .

Joining an elite breed of independent women who travelled the world in the 1950s and 1960s, Valerie lived a jet-setting life as an interpreter, working in exotic places and rubbing shoulders with prime ministers and presidents. At the same time she was juggling a Swiss chalet home, three children and a love-rat of a husband back in Geneva. But whatever Valerie did, she threw herself into it with zest. From dancing flamenco to being kidnapped in Cairo, wooed as wife number 14 by an African president or falling for a passionate Pole, Valerie's tales from home and abroad make *A Foreign Affair* a lively, funny, utterly delightful memoir.